The Power of Positive Investment in Yourself

in Yourself

Positive Thinking

The Power of Positive Investment in Yourself

Contents

The Power of Positive Investment in Yourself

You have most certainly heard about the power of positive thinking even

in life. Essentially, this is a theory that suggests that if you believe positive

things will happen to you, there will be a sort of the cataclysmic change in

the forces that affect you, resulting in really good things happening to

you. For how many people think about the power of positive thinking, you

will encounter many more who believe like it's all a bunch of pushing

Modern Age pop psychology or even sugar-coated Peter Pan platitudes.

There's a kicker here they're okay.

You know a system of convictions is positive thinking. So if you think it

doesn't work, then it won't work of course. Then if you find that it works...

yeah, you get the idea. For non-believers, it is like trying to find a career

after high school by using positive thinking. To get a career, you need

experience, but to get experience, you need a job. It can be hard to know

where you should start. But the key to making positive thinking work for

you is to start small, just like any other process. If you can, sow seeds, and

then learn how to grow and nurture those seeds until you have, year after year, a mental garden that bears a phenomenal harvest. With optimistic thinking, it is possible... even though you do feel it's all a bunch of crap.

Norman Vincent Peale, the founder of positive thinking, once said: "You attract zest and excitement if you have zest and excitement." Existence offers back in kind The essence of positive thinking is this." It's not so much a hypothesis as it's a disorder that's infectious. And as frustration and negativity spread rapidly from individual to individual, so do laughter and happiness-only positive emotions spread even more quickly. Think about it Have you ever found that cracking a joke is the best way to ease a stressful situation? A feeling of relief passes through everyone in the vicinity the moment anyone laughs or smiles. Even if the upset parties don't feel better, they should at least address the topic in a detached and rational way, instead of focusing on negativity, and get on with their lives. For the same intention, for at least the remainder of the journey, lone drivers who get cut off in traffic prefer to stay frustrated because there is no one else around them to give out positive vibrations and break the tension. Makes sense, does not it?

If you've picked up this book and read it so far there are still seeds of conviction. Your next move is clearing the garden of doubt in your mind and getting ready to plant. You will learn how to take all the negative into fertilizer and mulch it down to make your possibilities develop.

Grab your shovel now and let's go to the garden.

PLANTING SEEDS

In each phenomenon, the beginning remains always probably the most important moment.

- Thomas Carlyle

You should start tiny to tune in to the power of positive thinking, particularly if you don't believe it would work. One thing is to say to yourself, "Tomorrow, when I wake up in the morning, I'm not going to snooze a dozen times and feel sleepy for the rest of the day and another thing is to say to yourself, "Tomorrow, when I wake up in the morning, I'm going to be living independently wealthy and living in a mansion." (Unless of course at the moment you are currently independently wealthy and living in a mansion; in which case, you are independently wealthy).

The Power of Positive Investment in Yourself

For you, the process of making positive thinking work starts with destruction or at least a minor change in the structure of thought. You must first rip out all the old habits of negativity you've been creating throughout your life to make room for new approaches and concepts. For others, this will be an incremental process: you can eventually flush away the good-things-only-happen-to-other-people feelings when you watch constructive thinking work for you, one little step at a time, and be able to nurture the seeds of improvement.

Roots: What has your Garden Now?

The best revolution of the generation of ours is the discovery that man, by changing the internal attitudes of the minds of theirs, can easily alter the exterior features of the lives theirs.

- William James

What holds you back? Those who thoroughly support the philosophy of positive thinking can feel some discontent about entrusting their lives to mere thinking. Several options in your mental garden could grow weeds, and the only way to get rid of a weed is to yank it out, roots and all. We will address some of the most popular stumbling blocks people face on the path to positive thinking in this segment, as well as how to resolve them and set the groundwork for a healthier outlook on life.

Self-Esteem: dealing with the "I-Love-Me" Disease

Self-esteem was an unheard-of concept for much of human life, akin to the ideas of those heretics who thought the universe was round. During the '60s and 70s, the word "self-esteem" - described by Webster's Dictionary as "pride in oneself; self-respect" - found its way into the mainstream public consciousness as a catch-all term to capture the root of parenting issues. The "old ways" of parenting were declared cruel and detrimental to our youth's burgeoning self-esteem, and many parents afraid of raising depressed, ill-adjusted kids took the advice that contributed to a generation of kids with high self-esteem... so high that personal obligation was eclipsed and a "me-first" mindset was developed.

Exactly where do you rate on the self-esteem-o-meter? The following quiz is going to help you gauge your feelings and determine areas that need improvement.

Much of us on the other hand, are told that a vain, greedy, and unhealthy tendency is to think highly of ourselves. Advice that tells us to feel better for ourselves and even putting ourselves first is at best counterintuitive.
The Power of Positive Investment in Yourself

After all, is the first move on the path to Ego Central, not self-love? Many people want to feel positive about themselves but shame rears its ugly head too much and prevents the production of positive self-esteem.

Self-esteem is a difficult little emotion to exploit owing to these opposing perspectives. Striking a balance between modesty and greed is necessary. It takes practice to persuade yourself while bearing in mind that you are not the core of the universe, that you are a worthwhile and deserving person. While it can seem difficult, it's easy to do.

Where on the self-esteem-o-meter do you rate? The following questionnaire will help you assess your emotions and recognize places that require adjustment.

Me-ology: The Self Esteem Dipstick

Choose the response that most closely represents your probable reaction to the following circumstances to score your self-esteem:

1. You know that you're fantastic at database formation. Your employer asks a volunteer to organize a new consumer knowledge database for you and several co-workers, and another volunteer to write a business newsletter, which you have no idea how to do. You: You:

A. Volunteer for both, and you're so smart, you'll be able to work it out - including the first few times you write a bad newsletter at the risk of embarrassing the organization.

B. Database volunteer-and when Fred Jones volunteers as well, politely point out that you've got more experience, so you'd be able to show him what you know as you go along with it.

C. Remain in silence. Surely someone else is better at it than you are and the manager will never choose you either.

2. You're out with friends and in the middle of a pub, you've just passed gas noisily, so you:

A. Blame a passing waiter or someone else at your table instantly. In your allegations, you're serious, and there's no way that anyone can put it on you. You'll let them have it if they even think about it.

B. Crack a joke about the lunchtime four-bean salad you got.

C. Try to crawl under the bench, then excuse yourself, then go to the toilet. For the remainder of the night, you can't face either of them because right now you're debating paying the whole check

and leaving before they notice you're gone—if they notice you're

gone.

3.   When you watch or play Trivial Pursuit on Jeopardy, you:

A.   Laugh at the other teams if they have the incorrect answers. You

know both of them and you'd wipe them out if you ever go on

Jeopardy.

B.   Only laugh. You know a couple of the answers and you're trying to

guess the rest. You enjoy learning new material.

C.   Don't watch or play Trivial Pursuit on Jeopardy. For things like

that, you're not smart enough.

4.   After the promotion at college, you have chosen to go. You: You:

A.   Making a lot of other people look poor because you're not going

to get brushed by in any way.

B. Let your manager know that you are interested in the job, and then put some extra work into showing that you are fit for the position.

C. Decide that you are not going to go for it at all, on the drive to work. No matter what you do, you cannot get it, so there is no point in trying.

5. When making a difficult decision, you:

A. Pick the one that currently sounds better for you and then stick to your preference no matter what, even though it turns out to be the wrong one.

B. Before settling on your final decision, consider your choices and think about the benefits and drawbacks of each one, but stay open to compromise if it turns out there is a better approach.

C. Decisions? Rules? Decisions you can't make. You still do the wrong thing and end up leaving everyone wretched. You're going to get a decision from someone else.

6. You're left alone for a whole evening. You: You:

A. Gloat, so you don't have to waste time with those wretched

cretins who think they're mates of yours but they can't hold a

candle to your bright and dazzling personality. They all lounge

there, you know, hoping they could hang out with you anyway.

B. Take the opportunity to do something you love, like taking a long

bath, reading a nice book, or cooking your favorite meal for

yourself. It's good to rest and be alone with your ideas once in a

while.

C. All night, resign yourself to being sad. You may as well go to bed

early and pray that there's someone around tomorrow.

7. When executing a job that needs your total attention, you:

A. Don't. Don't. If it is that you do, you will do it in your sleep. You

don't have to mess about stressing about things.

B. They will tune out any obstacles and finish the assignment to the

best of their abilities. To put the best foot forward, you are

determined.

C. Can't. Can't. You're too stressed to focus on screwing things up, so you prefer to work in short bursts on assignments and sometimes end up doing things late because you're too busy.

8. You are introduced to someone new by a friend. You: You:

A. Show it by doing something funny or smart that lets them know your friend is paying attention to you right now not them, you're a nicer guy. If it is worth understanding the new guy, they will make the effort to get to know you.

B. Welcome him or her warmly, present yourself and ask an open-ended question like What are you doing to make a living?" "or Where are you living? You are prepared to listen to the response and will withhold judgment before you get to know the individual better.

C. Mumble 'hi,' and then slink off in search of a mate who doesn't chat to someone you don't know. They wouldn't want to get to know you anyway, whatever the new entity is.

9.   You walk into your house and you are met by a horrible smell: the fridge is unplugged, and everything that is in it is ruined. You: You:

A.   Automatically conclude that someone with it was screwing around and start an investigation to locate the suspect.

B.   To find out how it works, turn it back in first and then try to sort out what happened. If it is the duty of someone else to unplug it, they will help you wipe it out. You will, in any event, do what is required to fix the issue.

C.   You must have done something wrong, you decide, and now it's coming back to haunt you. As you vacuum out the refrigerator, you grumble under your breath and ask why things such as this still have to happen to you.

10. You're called into the office by your boss to congratulate you on the tremendous work you're doing on your latest project. You: You:

A. Thank him outwardly, he remembered how nice you are all the while realizing it's about time. Perhaps you'll get the recognition you deserve now.

B. They're genuinely flattered, and say so to him. You're just wondering if there is anything you can do differently.

C. Insist that you don't do all that well really just try to rush him up so that you can run. You should not warrant recognition.

11. You have to chat about a recent incident with your employer that impacts the way you and your co-workers do your job. You: You:

A. Behave as though you are best friends with your manager, and insist that she do something to resolve the situation. You could run the show almost as easily as her, after all, and you'd do a better job.

B. Approach the matter respectfully and with faith that there will be a solution. You give any ideas you might have to address the problem, and inquire if she has any views about what can be done.

C. I can never consider talking to your manager. She's the manager

for a cause and you're not. You could give her an anonymous e-

mail or invite her to speak to one of your co-workers.

12. You've got a hundred little tasks at home this weekend that have

to be completed, and you feel a bit stressed. You: You:

A. Strike many items, beginning from the simplest ones, at once. You

could not manage to complete all of them but since you have

more important things to do, you should still demand that

someone else pitch in.

B. Decide which tasks first need to be done and take them one at a

time. You will finish what needs to be achieved by doing it stage

by step. You'll ask them to help out if someone else is available at

home.

C. Bemoan the sad twist of fate that wrecked your weekend. There's

no way that you will ever complete it. You don't ask anyone else

for help, because they have other things to do than give you

favors. After all, you don't want to be an inconvenience.

13. For you to follow your dream career, the chance exists, however
that will mean quitting your new, secure position right away. You:
You:

A. Drop it all off and go with it. Who wants a net for safety?

B. Weigh your choices, and if the latest chance falls through, figure
out what you can do. You negotiate the decision with them and
create a contingency plan if you have a girlfriend. You will find a
way to make things work if it is possible.

C. Where you are, remain right. Why Disappointment at Risk? You
just know it's not going to work out.

14. You've got five minutes to get to a meeting, and you're stuck at a
dead stop in an almost relentless traffic jam. You: You:

A. Constantly swear, fume, and honk the trumpet. Do these people
not know that you are in a hurry?

B. They're upset, but you know that you can't do anything to change

the outcome. You call and let them know you're going to be a

little late if you have a mobile phone. To chill and listen to your

favorite radio station or just to remember, you use the

unpredictable moment.

C. The wish to die. Stuff like this tend to constantly happen to you.

It's just not fair. You're so nervous that you feel sick for being late,

and there's no way you can rest until you get out of this mess.

15. One of the tasks is checked by a co-worker and he advises you a

few items that are not fun, but they are valid points. You: You:

A. Thank him with your teeth clenched, then insist that you know

what you're doing. He has a lot of nerve to attack your

employment, and he doesn't even care for his beliefs anyway.

B. Thanks for the chance to better your career. Before handing it in,

you thank him for his insight and go back through the idea with

his ideas in mind.

C. Giving up. Nothing you will do better. Perhaps your co-worker,

instead of you, should have been in charge of this initiative.

You're probably going to mail it in and pray that you're not fired for misconduct.

Results: To figure out where you score on the self-esteem dipstick, count up all the A, B, and C responses:

Primarily A:

Place the mirror down, Narcissus. Your reservoir just overflows. You may not be aware of this, but you have way more confidence than you like. While trust is a good quality to possess, too much of it can make you look smug, rude, or unapproachable. Try to take better note of the thoughts of others, and you will go even further.

You have Great Harmony, join the Circus. Tempered with empathy and compassion for others, you have a good degree of self-esteem. You're probably the party's life or the one to whom everybody falls for support, and you're happy to give it when you can, however you know when you need your own time.

mostly C:

The Power of Positive Investment in Yourself

You'll end up in China if you search any further. You are a couple of quarts down, and you could use top-off self-esteem. You may think you can't do something right, but you'll find your worth even more than you think with a little confidence and some optimistic thinking. It's time for a full machine flush and refill if you have responded C to anything.

The Dark Ages: Past Letdowns and childhood Programming
Upon the kids of ours, the way they're taught rests the fortune- or fate- of tomorrow's world.

- B. C. Forbes

It's not easy to forget the lessons we experience in infancy—mostly because we don't consciously recall them. Subconscious thinking is much more challenging to dislodge. When we are ignorant not only of whether we accept or reject such things but also unaware of the fact that we embrace or avoid them, it is a complicated task to determine the origin of our acts.

Childhood lessons do not often come from our parents, and sometimes even the messages we received from them were not purposely put there. For starters, you might have learned those lessons too well if your parents taught you to be friendly, courteous, respectful, and giving, that the mere thought of doing things for yourself makes you cringe-and you may not know why. On the other hand, if your parents give you anything you wanted without even asking for it or raising your finger, you're going to be able to project the same demands on those around you—again with no idea whether you do it or even why you do it at all. Many times outwardly greedy people are surprised to learn that others view them as selfish. They might also assume that the kindest, most benevolent people they meet are themselves.

The external factors that shaped your development are another aspect you do not know while attempting to access your childhood programming. Whether knowingly or unintentionally, teachers, daycare staff or babysitters, school mates, and random people in the grocery store may have had an effect on your actions and values.

While all of your childhood experiences can be difficult to ascertain, you may give yourself a general sense of past events and behaviors that influenced your current values and take action to alter them. The accompanying short exercise will assist you to continue to learn about your causes and routines.

The Power of Positive Investment in Yourself

Exercise: Connect-the-influences

1. In a single column down the left-hand side of a sheet of paper, beginning with your parents, list the names of any person you can remember whom you interacted with during childhood. Use a short definition such as the lady at the end of the street with the loud little dog" if you don't know a person's name. Including families, colleagues, students, nurses, neighbors, and everyone else you recall. Tape another piece of paper to the bottom of the first one if you run out of space, and keep going down the left-hand side.

2. List all the behaviors and characteristics you exhibit, both positive and bad, on the right-hand side of the paper. Ask a mate to help you come up with some of the traits you possess that you may not be sure of if you feel courageous. You don't even have to show your list to anyone you can phone them up and remind them your New Year's goals are having a head start.

3. Now, will come the fun part. Make an effort to fit each habit or maybe trait with one of the individuals from the left-hand column, as well as draw a line to link them. You might find that some individuals have a number of connecting lines, while others

have none. Pay attention to the individuals that appear to have been seen on your list for no specific reason. If you recall them obviously, they most likely influenced your life in a bit of a little way.

The aim of this exercise is not to blame the people in your history for ruining your life. Instead, it is to demonstrate that all of your shortcomings and undesirable traits are the product of lessons that you have experienced as an impressionable child, and should thus be let go without remorse. Children view things from a different prism than adults do and all we do as grown-ups will sometimes end up coloring what we experience at an early age. Fortunately, as we approach them with the experience and rationality we have gained along the way, we will learn to let go of those negative impulses.

Taking back on the Horse

If you've made mistakes, possibly serious ones, there's usually another possibility for you. What we call failure isn't the falling down, but the staying down.

- Mary Pickford

The Power of Positive Investment in Yourself

You may have encountered failures or letdowns past infancy, about which you distinctly remember the rationale. We are also so resistant to change that the slightest hint that a fresh way of doing things doesn't work out becomes the warning to stop trying. We are creatures of habit, and it is a struggle to shake the pattern that we have built for ourselves that few believe they have the time or the resources to tackle.

Fortunately, before the cracks become large enough to break free, we may chip away at that mold. Breaking a pattern takes 21 days, according to most psychologists. In response to letdowns, the behaviors and responses you create are nothing more than patterns that you can rid yourself of with practice.

Ready to do a new exercise? Create a list of all the tasks you tried and started doing before you finished (remember, you didn't fail at them-you just made a temporary pit stop on the progress path). This list can include diets, commitments, workout routines, avoiding smoking, or even services such as this one for self-help. After each object, leave yourself some room. When you get to the end of the list, as a result of waiting to follow through, go back and fill in those patterns you have formed. For instance, if you discussed "The Atkins Diet," your habit may be "overindulging on pasta because for six months I have not eaten any." Some of your habits may be easy to change; others may entail a departure from your expected

course. You should remember that you can still eat pasta in the pasta

case, but not as much as you have been when making up for the loss.

With any habit, you can live with, come up with an alternative, so you

don't fall short before you get started.

You should start making meaningful improvements one step at a time

now that you have a map. Choose one or two patterns that you would like

to improve and make sure that the changes are enforced every day for 21

days in a row. To remind yourself of what you're working on and why

keeping a diary or a map is useful. With the satisfactory completion of

each habit-breaking period, you can even treat yourself to a reward. How

about a good big spaghetti plate? Go forward; you won it!

Where anything else does not deter us from accomplishing what we want

from life, anxiety moves in. In both aware and unconscious stages, we feel

anxiety and it is one of the most restrictive feelings we possess. Fear is

justified, and even safe, in some circumstances. An individual considering

crossing a busy street, for example, would have a healthy fear of being hit

by two tons of fast-moving steel widely known as a motor vehicle (at least

if he or she is a relatively sane person who knows the basic laws of

physics: moving car + walking person = splat). This fear induces caution, which prompts the entity to look both ways for traffic to come and wait for a good moment to cross the lane.

However, while fear is a factor, unjustified fear-which can be just as overwhelming and practical as justified fear-is more often the case. Daily, not many persons lose their lives. Humiliation, dismissal, and disappointment dominate the list of restricting fears of preparation and dedication that can be resolved.

**Currently, for most individuals, spiders dominate the list of their fears. The most prevalent form of fear in the world is arachnophobia—fear of spiders. Fear of spiders, though is entirely justifiable, since spiders are eight-legged creepy insects with fangs, alien eyes, and a propensity to drop out of nowhere on you. **

Exposure counseling, which is simply confronting your anxiety one small step at a time, is one of the simplest and most effective ways of coping with terror. If you don't feel like you can cope with exposure counseling alone, recruit a friend-especially if you can find a friend who isn't scared of the same things you're doing. In exposure therapy, the aim is to feel anxiety many times to a limited degree, so that it becomes easier to overcome each time. (Please remember that exposure therapy does not extend to any case, for example, it is not recommended that you jump from successively higher perches and aspire to become airborne if you are scared of flight, for example.)

For the Big Three fears, here are several ways you can incorporate exposure therapy:

Humiliation

- At the grocery store, wear your slippers. Scuff your feet over the floor and draw attention to your slippers if you're feeling ultra-brave. If you feel ultra-timid, go to a convenience store far enough away from your home that you'll never be seen again by shoppers.

- Sing at a pub of karaoke. And if you're sober.

- Choose one inappropriate piece of clothing (a Dr. Seuss hat, a large pair of mid-summer fluffy mittens, a bumblebee antenna headband) and wear it as long as you can in public. This is not just effective exposure therapy, it's fun!

- Enter a local Toastmasters club or volunteer to make a public lecture at a library or school on an area relating to your skills. Public speaking is an excellent way to exorcise shame, especially if you do it consistently (that's public speaking, not humiliating

yourself).

Rejection

- Dial-up a deejay at a radio station in a nearby country and order a Metallica or Ozzy Osbourne album. You may be laughed at and ignored, and there is a chance that you will be laughed at and rejected on the air. Be mindful that you may be rejected.

- If you are single, to locate an old school classmate you used to have a crush on, use an online location tool such as Classmates.com or PeopleFinder.com. Call them and ask (or just start a conversation) for a date. Ask an old school friend if you're married and invite them to lunch. They'll say no at worst; you'll get a pal rediscovered at best.

- Write a poem or short story and attempt to submit it or enter a literary contest in a newspaper or magazine. Become a writer automatically if you are not rejected.

Failure

- Try nailing Jell-o to a tree.

The Power of Positive Investment in Yourself

- Purchase a new video game and aim to win it in one sitting. Buy a video game that's different than the ones you normally play if you play video games daily, for example, consider a quest-driven style if you like combat video games. Or video chess.).).

- Start a new hobby that involves the production of an end product, such as weaving, design of model sets, or decoration of the cake. Please remember that it is not advisable to focus on cake-decorating exposure therapy to combat the fear of disappointment while you are focusing on your eating patterns. Your unsuccessful efforts will make you feel obligated to eat them. Try vegetable sculpture or arrangement of fruit bowls instead.

- Challenge Jeff Gordon to a car race in stock. As at least one of them is likely to happen, this will also help to conquer the feelings of failure and embarrassment.

By coming up with solutions to face your fears one small step at a time, you will decide your type of exposure therapy. Ask a friend to support you if you can't think of something. Many individuals are more than willing to learn something different, especially if they get to watch you do something fun.

The Power of Positive Investment in Yourself

NOTE: These activities are not meant to be a replacement for psychiatric professional treatment. You should seek the guidance of a licensed therapist if your fears are extraordinarily high and conflict with everyday tasks or regular activities. In cases of psychologically debilitating or trauma-induced anxiety, self-induced exposure therapy may help minimize or alleviate natural fear, but should not be used.

Trauma: Breaking the Chains

"If you are going through hell, keep going."

- Sir Winston Churchill

Bad stuff happens to decent people. It's a living reality. Our ability for endurance in the face of trauma is one of the most remarkable qualities of human beings. On the planet, miraculous survival and regeneration are not occasional occurrences. Someone survives a disaster every single day. Each day despite previous pain, someone takes another step towards a better life. Life begins each day and we adapt. And because of that, we are richer.

Once again the recommendations in this section are not alternatives for licensed psychiatric treatment. Many individuals have, however, considered self-help to be helpful in relieving the burden of depression and gaining care of themselves. If you want to seek therapeutic support or start on a healing journey yourself, remember that anytime disaster touches you, you will break free and begin to live again. You don't have to let trauma keep you out of life from doing what you want.

To focus on liberating yourself from trauma, you can use either one or any combination of these strategies. If an approach leaves you unhappy, move on to another range.

Dramatization and awareness: "It could be worse"

For minor pain, laughing is always the best treatment sometimes. If you can calmly look at the situation, you will be able to laugh it off or at least arm yourself with ample wisdom to understand that you have got it good.

This strategy has two ways of doing it. The first is to use your creativity in a clear way. Imagine the trauma, and then imagine all of the ways it could have been worse. For starters, you could have bounced a check if you have a checking account, ended up having to pay the bank a fee, and had to delay paying all of your bills, or went without anything you wanted to buy. Now, imagine what would have happened if you had some checks bounced. Maybe there were some bills you had to put off. The impact of the snowball may have caused you to lose your car, or have your electricity turned off. Your debts may have spiraled out of sight, potentially leaving you homeless. * It's easier to keep losses in perspective when you consider the worst.

NOTE: Bouncing many checks and losing your control, your car, or your house is considered a big trauma for which dramatization is not always successful.

The second approach to dramatization and understanding of mild trauma is to study real situations where other people's lives have turned out differently than yours. You can scan for news stories online, or check the local library's archive of periodicals. Generally speaking, you will still be sure to locate cases of those that have had more problems than you, and they have survived—and so will you. You're still here after all. You can do more to help those with your position if you want to take this approach a step further. Make a gift to a particular case or a similar cause, or launch your group with a service program or fund drive. Taking action, no matter how slight, also helps to relieve the trauma-associated feelings of deprivation and helplessness.

The Power of Positive Investment in Yourself

For Your Eyes Only: Journaling to Release

It is one of the oldest rituals of humanity to maintain a journal or diary. In numerous pages inscribed with words that are mostly kept secret throughout the writer's life, and exposed only to contribute to the historical record, the opinions, feelings, and sentiments of centuries have been preserved.

Often the process itself of writing down past pain helps you to confront it more thoroughly and relieve the negative emotions involved with the incident for therapeutic purposes. A short-term program used exclusively for focusing on a single trauma may be the journaling process. If you keep a short-term diary, as a symbolic realization of your liberation from pain, you will want to burn or kill it at the end of the process. You may want to continue keeping a written record of your thoughts and feelings if you enjoy journaling.

There are several different ways you can take from your journal. Some of the more popular ones are below, but feel free to come up with your journaling type to meet your personal needs:

- ***Freeform thinking.*** Freeform writing is a tool used to jumpstart imagination for many writers and potential authors. Holding a free-form notebook is a fantastic way to reveal ideas you might otherwise keep from yourself, and it's an excellent starting point for beginners. The freeform writing directions are simple: just sit down with your choice of the journal and writing software, and begin writing. Don't care about pronunciation, pronunciation, or even coherence. Simply write down something that comes to mind. Try to do this for at least five minutes to allow time to fire up the emotional engines. If after five minutes, you don't feel like stopping, just carry on writing. One of the most therapeutic activities possible is regular freeform writing.

- ***memories release.*** For short-term journaling, this strategy is most useful particularly if you plan to symbolically ruin the journal when you're done. Journaling memory release is just as it looks like: you write down your pain experiences and any emotions associated with them and then release those painful feelings. Imagine they are on paper now, and thus not in your heart or mind anymore. For this purpose, when you are done with it is more successful to destroy the journal.

- ***Story-form therapy.*** If the pain of your life has been triggered by a single individual or group of individuals, alive or deceased, writing a letter or sequence of letters to them may be effective in transcending the trauma. You're never going to give them emails, but writing down what you would say to them in the tangible form if you did, on a personal level, is incredibly rewarding. To protect your privacy and add more kick to your scathing monologues, you should address letters to their names, or assign them inventive nicknames (Dear Jerk, Dear Friend-Stealer, Dear Scum of the Earth).

- ***Pictorial Journals.*** To express painful feelings, you can believe words are insufficient. You may consider drawing a journal instead if this is the case. Just like to keep a book, you don't have to be a good writer, you don't have to be a good artist to draw one. If it is stick figures, abstract scribbling, or completely accurate rendering, use whatever type you feel comfortable with. To bring something specific down on paper is the most essential phase in journaling because no one except you will ever have to look at it.

It can be just as critical to pick the correct journal as what you put inside it. The human mind is a strong thing, and our emotions and beliefs affect our actions incredibly. Here are some tips for finding a fitting journal for your self-guided therapy:

- Your journal should be representative of scale, layout, look and feel, either of your intentions or your personality. Take the time to find a publication that you love looking at and keeping. Permit yourself to pay a bit more than you normally will and stop bargains or discounts (unless what you're shopping for is precisely the one on sale). Attaching to your journal a marginally higher dollar amount than what you would pay for something like a standard school-grade spiral notebook provides a mental boost to the importance of your journal, which helps remind you that it is important to you what you put inside it. Invest in one with a lock if you don't want someone else to read your journal, no matter what.

- Choose an instrument for writing that you can use exclusively for your journal. A pencil is the poorest medium to use, except for a pictorial journal, since it conveys the impression of a transient condition that can be modified with an eraser run. The best choices are pens or markers. You should write in the form in which you are more relaxed, which helps you symbolically or substantively. They are available in ballpoint models or standard chisel-point and inkwell types. You can select an ink color you like, purchase a package of shimmer pens, pick up a novelty pen, or even get an old-fashioned quill pen. Make careful to use only the writing instrument you select for your journal, not for shopping lists or phone numbers.

- Unless you are writing about it, find a home for your journal and keep it there. It is an important step in your journaling routine to establish a permanent position for your newspaper-under the bed, on the top shelf in the wardrobe, in a dresser drawer, on your nightstand. This helps to improve permanence and build new patterns (and reduces the risk of missing your journal).

Meditation: Connecting Above Pain

Meditation is a time-honored method of healing that has been used successfully for decades in Eastern cultures to relieve tension and concentrate the mind. In the United States, this method has recently gained traction when millions of people learn both the effects of meditation for physical and mental wellbeing while discovering that it is not as complicated as it seems.

Meditation will help you recover the vitality that the depressive feelings zap and learn to live with the stress-related challenges of trauma applications. One of the simplest and cheapest ways of self-therapy is meditation: all you need is yourself and a quiet space.

There are some meditation variants that you can do. You can pick the steps or mix of steps in which you are most relaxed and use them daily. The above are only a few of the hundreds of ways of meditation in existence, or you can blend elements of numerous programs of meditation to create your special technique.

NOTE: The goal is to clear the mind of conscious thoughts in all types of meditation and focus on actually being in the moment.

Walking Meditation: You can both meditate and exercise while you practice walking meditation. You just focus on either the sensation of your foot touching the ground with each step or on your breathing, which should be calm and normal, to meditate while walking. It takes practice to gain focus to blank out thoughts, but the normal pace of walking provides the beginning meditation student with an excellent starting point.

Standing Meditation: Standing meditation is a good way to practice breathing correctly since a standing stance is conducive to correct balance

The Power of Positive Investment in Yourself

and fully open airways. Stand upright and securely with your feet facing upward, about a shoulder-length apart to perform standing meditation. Place your hands on your lower abdomen one over the other and focus on breathing. Before finally releasing, take deep breaths and keep for about four seconds. Both in and out, proper meditation breathing is practiced by the nose. Per your choice, standing meditation may be done with your eyes open or closed.

Seated Meditation: The most famous type of meditation is this. Be seated either in a comfortable chair with your feet flat on the floor in a silent space, or in a cross-legged position on the floor (usually Indian or Lotus). You should focus on breathing, as in standing meditation, and slowly clear your mind of thoughts. With calm, open eyes focused on a fixed position on the floor about three feet in front of you, seated meditation is carried out. "Most seated meditation practitioners use alternative focus stimuli (see "External Stimulation Meditation").

Reclined meditation: Reclined meditation is best done right before you decide to go to bed, as sometimes you fall asleep as you do it. This version, just lying down, is the same as standing meditation. For reclining meditation, the eyes are still closed. For persons who have difficulty falling asleep, this is a beneficial strategy.

External Stimulation Meditation: If you cannot (or would rather not) concentrate on breathing, you may try using an external stimulus to concentrate your meditation thoughts. A mantra is one traditional example of external stimuli: a word or phrase that is repeated during the meditation session, either loudly or quietly. Some of the more common meditation mantras, such as om or aum (OHM: no English translation); om mani Padme hum (OHM mah-nee pah-d-may HUNG: the lotus jewel); or Rama (RAH-muh: chant used by Gandhi), are Buddhist or Indian in origin. With a sense important to you or your trauma, you may even construct your motto. Candles or incense; ambient music or captured chants; fans or white noise machines; miniature fountains; or recorded sounds of nature, such as waterfalls, bird calls, or whale songs, are other natural factors used in meditation. As long as it is calming and enjoyable for you, you can use whatever you'd like.

Join the Club: Online and live Support Groups

You will be shocked to hear that there is probably a community network of people who have gone through the same thing and can speak to you about it some sort of tragedy has influenced your life. It's awkward to explain certain forms of abuse with someone who hasn't had the same experience. With that reality in mind, help groups are formed.

The Power of Positive Investment in Yourself

If your trauma is a typical one such as substance misuse, you will be able to join a live support group that meets weekly in your city. Most churches, neighborhood associations, and local publications offer directories of area service groups for the group's coordinators with meeting dates, addresses, and contact information. You might consider joining one if there are no live support groups in your region. At the local library or online, you can find suggestions for creating support groups.

Even if the help you are searching for is not so general, the internet has helped people to interact and join all over the world who would otherwise never have met someone else like them. There are online communities, forums, and private discussion groups that represent nearly any walk of life, from displaced homemakers and sexual assault victims to reformed ex-convicts. Through diligent study, you will find a supportive and welcoming internet group to share your trauma with and interact with someone who has not encountered a traumatic incident at a level that would otherwise prove challenging, or even unlikely.

Drop That Horseshoe: There's No Such Thing as Bad Luck

The Power of Positive Investment in Yourself

In the last seven years, have you broken a mirror? Have any black cats recently crossed your path? There are several things attributed to luck in virtually every society, in every part of the globe: the possibility of good or bad occurrences occurring, also known as destiny or fate. For some variety of apparently unexplained situations, the chance is seen as a rationalization. "It is said that a gambler winning game after game at a casino table is "riding a lucky streak" (although his winnings can probably be attributed at least partly to ability); a homeless person is considered "down on his luck" (although there is almost certainly a concrete, though unfortunate situation behind his tragic state); a person for whom things always seem to go right is attributed "the luck of the I"

Many belonging to the philosophy of luck and following superstitions such as ignoring the number 13 and throwing salt over the left shoulder as it spills would insist that it works. It works for them, but this is merely a tribute to the ability of the imagination to compel us to do what we want to do. In much the same way as good thinking, chance works. You would be protected if you consider you are "safe" because you stop opening umbrellas in the house and going under ladders. On the other hand, if you crack a mirror and persuade yourself that bad luck is meant to infect you, you can subconsciously sabotage yourself and therefore draw bad luck-or at least, instead of discovering what happened, chalk up tragic occurrences to the shattering of the mirror so that you will keep the issue from repeating. Seven years is a long time to wait for an improvement in your fortunes.

Why not consider positive thinking, instead of rubbing the bellies of pregnant women or trying to catch heads-up pennies floating around? The same outcomes will be accomplished, except you won't have to rely on four-leaf clovers to be found or stop walking on sidewalk cracks. It's as straightforward to use the influence of optimistic thinking as knowing that good things will and will happen to you. To attract pleasure and prosperity, you don't have to memorize a specific series of laws or pursue intricate routines. So toss your lucky high school tee shirt and tap in today to think positively. Your probation for ill-luck is formally discharged.

Change The Mind, Change your Life

Many people are about as satisfied as they make up the minds of theirs to be.

- Abraham Lincoln

The most crucial move when tapping into the power of positive thought is to build a mentality that helps you to think positively. You will continue to plant the seeds that will anchor your new way of living after you have pulled the weeds from your mental garden.

It needs the training to develop a healthy attitude. You should train the mind to maintain positive thinking in about the same way that runners train their body to tolerate lengthy stretches of prolonged exercise and inevitably defer to fun or hopeful routes. Thinking positively at first can sound uncomfortable or absurd (particularly if you're the sort of person who thinks that people should be fired in the morning). Bear in mind, however, that the longer you do it gets better, and finally, keeping a good mentality would be as normal as breathing.

There are strategies you should take, like any fitness method to achieve your desired results: a constructive mental disposition in this situation. You can know that developing a new habit takes 21 days (what's that you've already forgotten? Go back and add "long-term memory" to your list of behaviors you'd like to improve). Therefore, for at least 21 consecutive days, you should perform each of the steps. You can take one move at a time or follow the whole program; just make sure you don't miss out on anything.

Step up and let the exercise begin on your mental treadmill!

The Power of Positive Investment in Yourself

Warm-up: ShakeOut Negative Kinks

When you think about it it's obvious: the negative is the opposite of the positive, so you ought to get rid of negative feelings to instill a positive attitude. That sounds easy enough, huh? The method is a simple one, but to make it stick, it takes practice.

To truly pay attention to your emotions is the first step in clearing negativity from your mind. Whenever the terms can't, shouldn't, wouldn't, won't, won't, or never cross your head, reflect on what you say and turn it around to remove the derogatory wording. For instance:

Your spouse and kids have been out for a couple of hours, and you have a spot for yourself. You engage yourself in one of your favorite hobbies. You appear to feel guilty in the middle of your happiness. You're thinking: I just shouldn't do this. I may be launching a project I promised someone else I would take care of. Your enjoyment begins to diminish, and you quit what you're doing, resentful that when you have too little time for yourself, you have to pursue this tedious project...

The Power of Positive Investment in Yourself

Does it sound similar here? The minute you catch yourself saying you're not supposed to, pause right there and change direction. In this case, you might think I really ought to be doing this instead. It's important to take time for myself, and I'll be able to do a great job on the project I told everyone else when I'm comfortable and happy. I'm so grateful that I have a chance to do something that I love.

Any time a bad thought creeps in, consider doing this. The more often you banish bad thoughts from your head, the easier it will become to think positively. For constructive solutions, you would feel more comfortable and receptive.

Work Those Mouth Muscles

If an image is worth a thousand words, then a million is worth a smile. A smile's strength is unbelievable. The simple act of lifting the corners of your lips, even though you don't feel like smiling, will make you lift your whole spirit and find something worth smiling over. Many who promote "fake it until you do it" have some of the best self-help tips out there This is particularly true when it comes to motivational reinforcement because faking a grin goes a long way towards creating the real thing. You may end up laughing at yourself only because you know there's nothing you have to smile for.

The Power of Positive Investment in Yourself

Another wonderful thing about smiles is that they're incredibly infectious. In daycare, a grin spreads quicker than a cold. When anyone throws a joyful smile their way, most individuals can't resist smiling back. This is a hypothesis that is clear and fun that you should try for yourself. Go to some public area and start smiling at unknown persons, so keep track of how many smiles (even suspicious smirking counts!) are coming back. You'll find that 9 out of 10 of your goals offer a small amount of your cheerful emotion back, and you've probably just made your day a little happier, too.

In cultivating a consistently happy outlook, learning to smile on demand is an essential step. Choosing a cheerful memory that never ceases to flood you with positive emotions is one good tool for summoning smiles. At the front of your internal catalog, keep this recollection and trigger it if you sense a blues case coming on. It does not fix your issues, but at least it will make you smile, which in turn allows you to relax and look at your situation positively. Smiling also provides the base of optimistic thought a mental prompt and helps to prime the pumps of satisfaction.

You should even spend a little time studying your gestures in front of the mirror. This practice can sound awkward or downright foolish at first but smiling at your reflection has a positive influence on your psyche. The delighted smirk; the close-lipped leg-pulling smile; the toothy grin; the laugh-out-loud open-mouthed smile: you should also practice multiple smile combinations. Think of it as an Olympic event... it's your own personal Smile Marathon, and every time you win gold!

Do some REPS

The value of repetition should not be understated when cultivating a healthy mentality. Exercise is the secret to constructing every muscle, so you can create a pool of happiness that can take you through the most grueling events by seeing your positive outlook as a muscle.

This is not to suggest that there is nothing you can care about. Ignoring unsettling things won't make them go anywhere. Facing your concerns and looking at them from a constructive lens is crucial. Your problems should not remove the good mentality itself. It is simply a tool to help you to find a solution through stress and anxiety without burning yourself out. When you can stand back and look at the situation in a better way, you can find it much simpler to solve problems; and sometimes the answer will show itself with little effort, simply because the mind is free and open enough to notice it.

The Power of Positive Investment in Yourself

The more you practice constructive thinking, the more it will come to you more easily. You will find that daily stressful incidents decrease to mild nuisances, and finally, cease to bother you altogether. Keep practicing constructive thinking methods, and you will be well on your way to a lifestyle of low stress and high energy that will allow you to do everything you want.

Cool-Down: Feel the Burn

Look back and focus on your success as you get to the close of your everyday constructive mindset exercise. Is there something about you that seemed easier? Were you able to find a simpler solution to a dilemma that would usually have taken up a lot of worrying time? Will you feel more comfortable and eager for tomorrow to try again?

Congratulate your victories on your own. You continue to build the foundation of your current optimistic outlook and pave the foundations for your future by enhancing your achievements. Optimistic thinking gets you to your ultimate target one step closer. Soon, you will know that you can do this, and as you continue, you will have an even stronger passion.

The next step is to learn how to look after your emotional farm, now that you've planted the seeds for constructive thinking. You will discover the fuel you need to cultivate your seeds in the next chapter and coax fresh shoots from your mind's dirt. Meanwhile, proceed to pump the iron with good thinking!

Terminals Switch: Hook Up to Constructive Energies

"No pessimist has ever discovered the secrets of the stars, or sailed to an uncharted land, or opened the human spirit to a new doorway."

—-Helen Keller

Enthusiasm is the sunshine of a garden in your head. Possessing a passion for everything you do is crucial to the positive thought process. Much as plants need sunshine to thrive and expand, it takes excitement to energize the ability and guarantee an unlimited supply of fuel to use the power of positive thought.

You'll find that the more momentum you create; the more energy you're going to have to bring in. It would be quick to create curiosity about certain items, and others where you will have to stretch yourself to discover what will ignite your enjoyment. Nobody has difficulty creating a passion for enjoying an unusual work bonus or taking a night out for instance. You may find it tough, though to get enthusiastic about washing dishes or filling out the income tax forms. Yet part of the magic of positive thinking is developing the desire in any situation to find the nice stuff and use it to get past the bad parts.

Enthusiasm must be cultivated and protected from potentially destructive stress storms, much as cultivating a healthy attitude. To add a shot of passion into everything you do, there are many strategies you can use, whether it's having your dream holiday or scrubbing out the basement. You should pick the strategy that best matches any situation you face to make sure that you have the stamina to handle everything that life happens to throw at you.

What's there for me in it?

Focusing on the gain you will obtain from performing a given assignment is one of the most elementary solutions for finding excitement. It's quick to discover the gains of certain cases. For e.g., you may dislike wrapping gifts, but when faced with this beautiful paper-wrapped package, you know the person you are offering the present would be overjoyed, and so you draw pleasure from envisioning the recipient opening the present. This is a particularly effective technique when you're already awake at 2

The Power of Positive Investment in Yourself

a.m. Trying to find out how to wrap up the bike you've just spent three hours putting together on Christmas eve.

Some situations are not going to have any apparent advantages. It would certainly be difficult to see the silver lining if you were to find yourself struggling to repair a flat tire on the side of the road in the middle of a snowstorm (or a rainstorm, if you are lucky enough to live in a snow-free climate). Permit yourself to dream about the wildest advantage you may come up with within stressful conditions. You may have been on the way to a party that you would like not to go to. Your flat tire would give you the best reason for turning around and driving back home in that situation.

In any case, there is something positive, whether it's in the form of a benefit or a lesson to be learned (Lesson One: Never drive to a party you didn't want to attend in the first place with dubious tires in a snowstorm). The power of positive thought can be harnessed by discovering and leveraging the good, no matter how slight or trivial it can sound.

The Buddy System

The Power of Positive Investment in Yourself

Try to find someone who loves doing that kind of thing and encourage them to work with you if you're having trouble summoning passion for a certain mission. Enthusiasm is infectious, much like laughing. Part of it is likely to rub off on you if you spend some time watching the passion of another human.

Try to go online to look up posts or blogs (weblogs, which are typically confidential, frequently published online journals) relating to the topic if you don't know someone who would be excited about what you're trying to do. Even only thinking about the excitement of someone else will help you find every part of the job to love, and with a minimum amount of tension, fear, and apprehension, get you through it. (Be warned: it might be hard to find someone who likes scrubbing toilets or emptying cat litter boxes. You may be on your own in these instances!)

Knowledge is Power

When you don't know what you're doing, muddling through a complex job or mission can be overwhelming. If you are the kind of person who never asks for guidance or reads notes, in places where your experience is minimal, you can be tempted to take on challenges. And if you're not, you may be faced with taking on a job that you don't feel prepared to manage, if it's standing in at work for someone in another department or changing the diaper of a child for the first time.

The better you know what you do, the easier it would be to achieve. This can sound self-explanatory, but many individuals don't know that more knowledge will still be sought. It takes just a few minutes to look up something on the internet, review a guide book, or contact someone you know who has experience with the problem you're having.

Information acquisition has other advantages as well. The more you know about a particular subject, the more you will be able to concentrate and work towards your target. If you cannot find the road, you cannot reach your destination. As the pruning shears of your mental yard, look at awareness, clearing the way for passion to expand and spread. You can complete any task quickly with the right collection of resources.

On the Dotted Line symbol

To create a sense of excitement, being committed to achieving your target is important. You should be committed to what you are trying to do whether you wish to have glowing white teeth or flash your pearly whites at hundreds of thousands when you receive your Academy Award.
The Power of Positive Investment in Yourself

A step-by-step roadmap for the accomplishment of your goals is one way to cement your professional dedication. No matter how large or tiny, you can do this for any job (although you might save time with stuff like washing the dinner dishes and build a mental schedule, as it would take you more time to write it all down than it might wash them). Note the starting point on a sheet of paper, or for monumental challenges such as shifting occupations, at the beginning of a notebook: where you are now. Leave some room for yourself and then jot down where you want to be and how long you are going to take to get there. Then go back and break down, in thorough stages, the method of going from point A to point B. Not only does this help you envision the completion of your goal, but it also helps you to mark measures off when you accomplish them. When you drive forward toward your target, your passion can be maintained.

Try forming a deal for yourself to accomplish that goal when you're writing it down. You may also ask to serve as a witness to a friend or family member, which will help reinforce your intentions to follow through. Your contract can be a straightforward text outlining a commitment to yourself or a comprehensive map of the tasks you can do to help yourself accomplish your goals, with deadlines for extra encouragement and bursts of excitement. To remind yourself of your intentions, keep your contract visibly posted. You'll find yourself ready to accomplish your goal and satisfy your deal any time you see it.

Dangle Yummy Carrot

Ask any company owner and you'll find out that one of the most potent motivators is incentives. If they know they will get more out of it in the end, people are more likely to work for a target. Because your boss obviously won't thank you for losing weight or remodeling your bathroom, when you reach a given goal, you should prepare to reward yourself.

Be sure to align them to your milestones when choosing self-rewards. Not only can this mean that you do not get bored with the same incentive, but it will also assist you as you prepare the tactics you can use to achieve your goals. For starters, you can treat yourself to a ticket to the cinema to see a wonderful movie if you would like to spend less time watching TV and more time outdoors or with your family. If you're trying to stop smoking, it might be part of your policy to put aside some of the money you're hoping to save by not buying cigarettes and having a new wardrobe for yourself or something you've got your eye on for a while but you can't afford it.

The Power of Positive Investment in Yourself

Any milestones come with inherent incentives that are already built-in,
yours for the argument when you hit your target. If you're going to start
your own company, for instance, you already know that you're going to
be paid by working for yourself, or even by working out of your house.
Whether you're working for an inherent benefit or giving yourself an
opportunity, a perfect way to create motivation for the job at hand is to
treat yourself.

Surrendering

That is right. You should just give up occasionally.

This might not be the sort of guidance that you would hope to read about
positive thinking in a novel. There is a special moment, though, that you
can surrender-and that is when you hate doing what you do.

"Just like what you're doing. Do something else if you don't like it.

- Paul Harvey, Paul Harvey

Very many people end up settling for the life they feel they should have
the life they have been encouraged to accept from others or the life they
think they are trapped with. You have to remember that there is room for
everybody on this earth and whether you feel stuck in a career that you

dislike or a living space that you can't bear, you have to make a change—not down the line, or when you have time, or whatever it is that you've been waiting for but right now. In the future, the mysterious "someday" will always be, because you can't keep up with the future. The only opportunity you have is now.

This doesn't mean that at least, not in most situations, you should abandon anything and throw caution to the wind. You have obligations that must be taken care of if you're like other people. Nevertheless, right now, there is always plenty you can do to cast your net out and grab "someday," and start dragging it towards you. Do you hate your work, nor do you lack the skills to get another one? Start to take lessons at night or sign up for an online course. Distance learning courses are provided over the internet by hundreds of approved colleges. Is your house or apartment in a neighborhood that started wonderfully, but every day gets worse—and you haven't found the time to move or the money? Take a careful look at your budget to see if for a few months there is something you can do without or ask your landlord or bank if they have any other assets that you might look at.

Waiting for fuels apathy's flames. Doing something about your condition will launch a chain reaction of motivation, no matter how slight or trivial it can seem, which can energize you to accomplish your goals. If you are always here to live it, you deserve to get what you want out of life. Don't put it off another day because right now your "someday" is!

SHOOTS AND LEAVES

"Motivation is the thing that gets you started. Habit is the thing that keeps you going."

- Jim Ryan

You will continue to see the signs of development of yourself and your surroundings now that you've planted your mental garden. At this point, the tender new beginnings of your optimistic, hopeful self are vital to nurturing. You should learn to consider the implications of positive thoughts in your life and promote the formation of deep roots to anchor yourself in results.

Tenacity aids.

Your Spring of Regeneration the First Signals

"There is only one corner of the universe that you can be sure of improving, and that is your own."

The Power of Positive Investment in Yourself

-Huxley Aldous

You will find that things continue to improve for you when you start practicing positive thinking. Perhaps the transition is so incremental that you don't feel it at all until someone else tells you one day that you look different. They could inquire if you had a new wardrobe, changed your hair, lost weight, or won the lottery.

Not only does it make you happy, but it also makes you more appealing by tuning in to optimistic thinking; the type of person you want to be around.

You might know some of the typical indicators of positively charged individuals now that you've had some experience. Check out this list of stuff that you need to look forward to.

You're a positive thinker when:

- Your grueling trip to work goes by so fast, you wonder why in the first place it ever worried you.

- The grocery store clerk gives you the incorrect change, you point it out with a grin, and she corrects the error happily.

The Power of Positive Investment in Yourself

- You waited twenty-five minutes in line at the bank for lunchtime... and your life didn't stop.

- After a week of the backorder, the latest part for your car landed at the garage, but it was the wrong one. When the garage called, you were so sweet about acknowledging the wait that they gave you a big discount on your maintenance bill.

- You grin every time you catch a glance of yourself in the mirror, and you don't think you look like a fool.

- You put the oven on your dinner so hot and burnt... and you ended up with something much better than you'd expected.

- You now have a lot of spare time and a lot of things to do with your hands, plus the stamina to do them.

- The last time you felt the word couldn't be in the expression, I couldn't believe all these wonderful things were happening to me.

Positive thought has the ability, as long as you believe it does to transform your life. You will find you don't have to invest any thought into doing what you desire if you continue to use constructive thinking strategies.

Conspiracy Theory: The greatest Threat to the New You
"When a male points a finger at another person, he must recall that 4 of the fingers of his are aiming at himself."
The Power of Positive Investment in Yourself

- Louis Nizer

Any road has its impediments. You can find only one of them in the path to healthy thinking: yourself. Human beings strive to construct conspiracies toward themselves and place on every part of their life the self-limiting values that affect them, whether those oppressive expectations derive from the environment, schooling, or a mixture of influencing influences.

Your self-defeating acts cannot yet be noticed. However, it is only inside yourself that the ability to access the rewards of positive thinking lies because you are the only one that can stand in your way. You must also learn how to step aside and allow yourself to grow to your full potential.

Some of the most common self-limiting conduct trends follow, along with actions you may take to get out of your way and blaze your road to peace and achievement.

There is Always Tomorrow: Eradicate Procrastination

"To be regularly intending to create a better and new life but hardly ever get time to set about it's as... to place off drinking and eating and sleeping from 1 day to the next until you are dead."

The Power of Positive Investment in Yourself

- Og Mandino

Procrastination is the simplest thing to perfect in the world and one of the most daunting practices to crack. Whether it's vacuuming the living room carpet or taking the European holiday you've been planning for years, there will still be a compelling excuse to put off everything you want to do.

One of the best things you can do anytime you know you are putting something off is to remind yourself why you don't want to do it. As diverse as the individuals who do it the motives for procrastination are the job is tedious or repetitive; you are worried that you will not be able to do it the assignment is challenging or time-consuming; it will be an uncomfortable experience; you fear the potential repercussions of seeing the task through to completion. You will decide the plan to reach your target and get un-stuck until you realize what stops you from going on.

How are you going to crush procrastination in its tracks? Remedies to get beyond procrastination include the following:

Simply do so. Whatever the mission you're facing, just choose a point and get started. Things are always not as bleak as they sound, and it's easier to build up momentum until you start doing something that can take you on to the finish. Tell yourself that you will not have anything hanging above your head until you end the difficult job and you can move on to other things.

• Split things up, individuals. To split up bigger objectives into short, manageable targets, take a few minutes. For example, if you're trying to organize your desk at work, before returning to the next drawer, you could select one drawer to get that done, and then take a break to do something else. It is more motivating and rewarding to achieve a set of small milestones than having to tackle a big project all at once.

• Cut the fluff through. When you are taking on a mission, train yourself to work through distractions. Avoid the phone, if possible, and certainly, fight the temptation to play Solitaire or update your e-mail hundreds of times. Be sure that your mind is made up to do whatever it is that you do and nothing else before it is done. You're going to feel comfortable thinking that this is completed, and you're going to spend less time on sideline tasks.

• Stick to the schedule. Ensure that you have enough time to complete the mission that you are beginning. If you know you're going to be distracted or run out of time before you're through, instead of having to hurry through the entire thing, pick one part of the assignment to finish. Rushing knows you can't cause more tension to reach a deadline, which can simply make things happen slower because you're afraid you're not going to be able to do what you've set out to do.

Expect the unanticipated. Things sometimes take a turn for the unexpected, amid our best constructive thinking efforts. Delays in certain cases are a given. It is important to factor in time while you are planning a mission or target in case something goes wrong. Delays are a major facilitator of procrastination: because you still have to hesitate, it is easy to persuade yourself to push something off. Be sure that you have a contingency plan in place so that you can stop putting things off and easily still achieve your completion targets.

Simply Say No: How to not Take On Too Much

"The greatest executive is the person who has sense enough to choose males that are great to do what he wants to be done, and self-restraint adequate to help keep from meddling with them while they do it."

- Theodore Roosevelt

The Power of Positive Investment in Yourself

People will still want you to do stuff for them. Existence is that. We are frequently asked to make obligations that we don't feel good with, have no time for or simply don't want to make, but telling "no" makes us feel much worse than committing to something that we don't want.

Women fell victim to the phenomenon of over-commitment. You can make it a habit to say "no" more often, particularly when you know that it would wreak havoc with your life to agree to take on a certain responsibility, even if the little voice in your head tells you that agreeing will be the "nice thing to do. The nicest thing when it comes to your sanity is to guarantee that you do not over-extend yourself and end up completing a vast amount of tasks with substandard results.

In learning to say no, the first step is to consider which things you can agree to stick to and which things are all right to move away. Your interests should derive from this decision; the things that are important to you and your life. This is one reason why, when you are using the power of positive thought, it is important to specifically identify your objectives. Weigh each proposal against your priorities and determine if it will bring you forward or further away from your goals to consent to them.

The Power of Positive Investment in Yourself

There are many ways to say no without damaging feelings or making yourself seem inconsiderate as you get to a point where you must deny a submission. When you say no, be as frank as possible and you will be able to continue with a guilt-free conscience.

Need an apology? The top ten ways to say no nicely are here:

1. No The best way to refuse, sometimes is politely, but directly." A strong "no" is the best way to get them to quit if someone in your life is continually pressuring you to do something that they could easily do themselves. Another solution to troubled persons with repeated inquiries is to say I know you're going to do a great job handling it on your own."

2. "Right now I'm in the middle of several other projects/commitments." When you're distracted, don't be afraid to tell people. Many will value the timeline and find another way to satisfy their assistance demands. To complete new ones, you should not be forced to abandon projects you've already committed to.

The Power of Positive Investment in Yourself

3. "At the moment, I need to concentrate on [my career, my family, my personal life]." If you are going through a tough time in another area of your life that needs your attention, don't hesitate to refuse to consider additional requests. You may not have to justify your particular reasons for taking a pass; just show that you are taking a pass.

4. I don't believe I'm the right person to do the work." If you don't feel qualified to handle something that you have requested, say so." Explain why you don't want to do a bad job because you know that the person asking you to do so is vital for this mission. Chances are, they will want the assignment done properly.

5. I can't do it but I know someone else who can If you truly know someone who can not only handle the task but has the time to do it, use this "no" form only." It's good to be able to provide alternative assistance, but only if the offer can be carried through. It would be taken as a brush-off to send them to someone else who will not be able to help either the person who first came to you will believe you never really intended to help them in the first place.

6. "I don't feel comfortable/don't like to do that." Keep to your weapons. When you're asked to do something that appears to be unfair or to do a job that you hate, don't embrace it and justify why. You'll be able to stop repeated demands for the same thing this way.

7. "Right now, I can't help but ask me later." Again with this comment, be honest. If you just want to help out but don't have the time when the request is made, let the person asking you know that when you do, you will be glad to help out. Give them specific accessibility, if possible, like tomorrow or next week, when you know you're going to be accessible. They can find someone else if they need the assignment completed before then.

8. "I don't have any experience with this kind of task." This is equivalent to saying that you're not the right person for the role but more important for you at least. You shouldn't have to learn a whole new skill set when you work on a job with someone else just to complete one item. If it's something you wanted to learn

anyway though, you may want to take advantage of the chance to learn something new.

9. "I know you want the goal of another person], but right now I can't get away from another commitment]." This is a respectful way of acknowledging the other person's desires and refusing to overwhelm yourself. It will also open the ability for all of you to handle the root problem of the request in a manner that is easy.

10. "No, but If you can't agree to a proposal for some reason, you can suggest a solution that will be helpful to the case. You may not be able to undertake the exact job required, but you might be able to help out with another part of the project. Again without making you appear callous or unconcerned with whoever requests you, this leaves your choices open.

Whenever you're challenged to take on more than you know you can do, practice telling no both at home and work. It can be a hard habit to break to over-extend yourself, but it is a necessary step towards staying out of your way so that you can fulfill the goals of your life. You have your own time, and you must be accountable for ensuring that your interests are fulfilled.

The Power of Positive Investment in Yourself

Take Me as I Am: Kicking the Approval Habit

"You can't be lonely if you love the individual you are on your own with."

- Dr. Wayne Dyer

Everyone needs validation from those we care for and recognition. Too much though, we focus so heavily on the acceptance that we lose sight of the most significant approval of all: our own.

Can you hear yourself just agreeing to stop disagreeing? Before you make a decision, are you always asking for the support of others? This addiction to recognition is counterproductive to your quest to better your life by a positive thought. You become less focused on your thoughts and emotions by feeding your acceptance habit, and thus less in tune with your objectives and what is better for you. The only person you can make happy one hundred percent of the time is you, even though it's great to have the support of other people.

How do you kick the habit of validation and stop thinking about what other individuals think about your actions? To ensure that your people-pleasing prowess is seen just when you intend it to be, and not as a crutch for social recognition, here are some action plans you should adopt.

The Power of Positive Investment in Yourself

Know the Secret

You ought to recognize your values and principles to stop getting

acceptance for the sake of approval. Being mindful of what you believe

will help you express your beliefs and take the best direction for yourself,

even though others do not agree. It is a necessary part of the process of

positive thought to build a good moral code.

It will help to reinforce your values and principles and act as a reference

for your decision-making process by writing down your moral code.

Dream of the concerns that are vital to you. Will you agree that family

values come above anything else? Is it important to you for your career?

Where do you stand with politics: would you like to be outspoken about

your views, or attempt to make a difference by voting in the background?

In any case, a moral code should control your acts, and you should never

betray your values just to obtain someone else's approval.

It can be an integral part of taking care of yourself and your life to stand

up for what you believe in. You become a better person when you avoid

wanting acceptance or affirmation for any of your opinions because ideas-

and the people who care for you will love and appreciate you for it instead of walking away. Be aware of the moral code and build it and adhere to it. You're going to be shocked by how much happier you feel about yourself... because you're not going to need someone else to second your view.

Middle School Graduation

The need for recognition started in high school for all of us. For most teenagers, the need to fit in is intense, and there is usually nothing more valuable than friends while you're in school. It can be hard to break the impression that you are only a worthwhile person if you have a lot of friends, or the "right friends until we leave the boundaries of school systems and join the adult world.

As adults, we need to discard our school days' petty social pecking order. Life is not a contest for fame. It does not surprise you to hear that social outcasts in school became the most popular adults. A major part of the reason for this is that they did not cultivate their peers' approval, they were able to engage in themselves, acquire experience and grow powerful identities that did not rely on the "in" crowd's affirmation.

The Power of Positive Investment in Yourself

In case you need evidence, check out the following list of accomplished individuals at the bottom of the food chain who suffered through high school:

- All of his peers called Henry Kissinger a little fatso".

- Voluptuous actress and model Heather Graham were regularly teased for being shy and underdeveloped physically.

- Walt Disney was considered a shiftless dreamer who by his teachers and classmates, would never amount to much.

- The owner of the NYC nightclub Suede, which is frequented by Britney Spears, Cameron Diaz, and Leonardo DiCaprio, Eytan Sugarman, was a chubby and polite boy whose guidance counselors advised him that his life would go nowhere.

As an adult, outside of high school, you are far more aware of understanding that peer recognition doesn't matter. To be true to yourself, you should aspire. Note, everyone has a place—and it's a huge world.

Weed Yours Garden of Friendship

The Power of Positive Investment in Yourself

Most of us from the number of friends we have, prefer to judge our worth. This is not necessarily a fair estimation, though, and keeping up with your lunch dates and Christmas card lists can be tiring—especially when you have friends with whom you can't be yourself.

To assess your friendships, take some time. Are there people with whom you spend time who tend to exhaust you while you're around them? When you communicate with them do you constantly feel like a fraud and watch the clock until enough time has elapsed, so you can excuse yourself from the conversation? Friends are great to have, so it's not worth cultivating any partnerships.

The next time you find yourself stuck in an unpleasant situation and are unable to share your true feelings, try to speak your mind instead. Either of two things is likely to happen: either the person you are talking to will be interested in your thoughts and you will feel the conversation going into actual territories, or you will experience a sudden drop in temperature and hear from the other person those reasons you normally make to avoid. If the case is the former, your friendship has changed and you can relax around the individual; if it is the latter, you have just got rid of an unwanted drain on your resources and positive thinking mechanism.

The Power of Positive Investment in Yourself

Nothing is wrong with terminating friendships that simply don't work out. Chances are the other person will be as relieved as you are, and the relationships you have with genuine friends will both be able to improve. It's going to take some time to remove the weeds from your garden of friendship, but it's going to be worth it for everyone involved. When you no longer have to "fake it" to get along with anyone, freeing yourself from damaging relationships helps you kick the approval habit.

Blood is denser than embarrassment

One thing is severing relationships with friends, and another thing is doing the same with family. Most of us are raised with the idea that family is essential, and we tend to be more forgiving of members of the family and more often seek their approval for our actions. We're afraid to be around family members, mostly because people change, and we're afraid that the changes that come into our lives won't please our close relatives. So we're forced to continue acting like we were five, ten, or fifteen years ago, the same people we were. This generates an uncomfortable relationship at best and if left unchecked, can lead to estrangement or avoidance.

The Power of Positive Investment in Yourself

Try to keep in mind that just as you forgive the collective flaws and personality quirks of your family members, they will forgive your own. When you care for someone based on their feelings, beliefs, and behaviors, you support them for who they are and don't criticize them. Why does your kin not apply to you the same courtesy?

It could be much more necessary to be yourself and not need permission from your family than to do so with peers. From our relationships with our families, we seem to derive the foundation of our degree of self-protection, and if we cannot be secure around the family, the sense of false security extends into all aspects of our lives. If you've shielded some part of your personality or value system from your family out of fear that they won't support you, try to eventually ease your own beliefs. You may be shocked to learn that you are more tolerant than you expect of the people who care for you. They may have practiced the same safe emotional pose often as you and maybe almost as glad when it's actually out in the open.

You don't need your family's permission for the things you want to do in any event. While excluding a family member from your life is more complicated, if including them is more dangerous, then you should try putting some space between yourself and the disruptive family member.
The Power of Positive Investment in Yourself

Many individuals are happy with deciding to disagree, and each of you will come to an understanding of time. Meanwhile, don't let the desire to be you outweigh the need for acceptance. Second, please, and no one else is going to do that for you.

The Blame Game: Whose Fault Is It, Anyway?

"The reason individuals blame items on the prior generation is there is just one other choice."

- Doug Larson

We are a blame-driven culture. We blame the establishment for running our lives, and our parents for ruining our lives. We blame the fast-food industry for making us obese, the nicotine industry for supplying us with cancer, and the system of justice for encouraging criminals to roam around us while innocent people remain in prison. Our kids are blamed for giving us grey hair, and our schools are blamed for equipping our kids with actions that make us old before our period. There is no wrong move, major or small, that we can't find someone else to apologize for. The last person we blame is ourselves.

The Power of Positive Investment in Yourself

Very much, however, as difficulties occur, we are the first one we can point to.

The government does make the rules-but we're in charge of choosing the rule-makers, and most of us don't vote, although most of those who do are under-informed. Our parents have a huge influence on our lives—but they can only raise us as well as their parents have trained them, and we are responsible for our actions until we become adults. When we break the rule, we tend to eat so much fast food, smoke cigarettes, and try and get away from prosecution. As living reflections, our children imitate our actions back at us and no matter how much of their time they spend in school, their behavior is almost entirely dictated by what we teach them at home.

It is up to each of us to be responsible for our lives. And if the wrongs of our lives are the responsibility of someone else, we are the one who controls our response to the situation. You can continue to get upset and point fingers when bad incidents arise in your life, or you can choose to do something about it. Be honest about who is to blame for your life's troubles, and take action to remedy the crisis.

The Power of Positive Investment in Yourself

Omelet Making: How to Learn from The Mistakes

"Remember only the last time you need to succeed."

— Brian Tracy

They all make mistakes. The good news is: loss will be good for you

honestly! By finding out ways not to do anything the easiest way-and

sometimes the only way to learn how to make improvements in your life

and accomplish your goals.

To learn from your mistakes, there is a process you can use. The more you

understand, the closer you will be in life to fulfilling your objectives.

Give Permission to Yourself

You know that you're going to make mistakes, particularly if you want to

do something you never did before. Force yourself even when you make a

mistake, it's always okay—and you won't let errors deter you—to be

prepared for the inevitability of mishaps and misadventures.

The Power of Positive Investment in Yourself

This is part of instilling a good attitude in the process. It's harder for surprises to set you back from your path to achieving your targets if you know what to expect. Bear in mind that making errors is all right, and doing so is not the end of the universe. The only ones who do not make mistakes are people who, first of all, do not want to do something. Don't be the person who regrets that you were scared of failures, never really attempting to reach your goals.

Create fascinating errors

Once again you will make mistakes. When this happens, by making fascinating errors rather than dumb ones, you can understand more.

Maybe you're curious what, precisely, is an interesting error? The more elusive and elusive your end objective is the more remarkable your mistakes would be. It is much more likely that the person who suffers a spectacular failure will attain spectacular success. Here's a short instance:

STUPID MISTAKE: Stubbing your toe on the rake lying in the yard that you left.

INTERESTING MISTAKE: Converting powdered sugar and chocolate chips worth $30 into inedible bricks when attempting to launch the candy-making business because the candy thermometer is misread.

When you're done with them the first error will teach you to put away your resources, but this is something you actually should have learned anyway. However, the second fault is much more important to you. It shows you how not to read a thermometer for sweets, and you will never make the same mistake. You are now one step closer to fulfilling your goal of starting a business that makes sweets. What's going to be the next error?

'Fess Up

The willingness to accept that you have made an error is vital to the process of learning. This does not mean that you have to reveal to the world your mistake. You do have, though to be frank about yourself. It is necessary to own up to your mistakes, not only in your efforts to learn from them but in the whole process of using positive thinking.

The Power of Positive Investment in Yourself

Be careful not to judge your acts unfairly when you confess your errors to yourself. It's not meant to be your feelings along the lines of I messed this up, and I'm never going to get this right. Don't let errors teach you not to try. Instead, I suppose I made a mistake, and now I don't know how to do it again. In taking responsibility for them and then doing something to fix what went wrong, you will find the best lesson in making mistakes.

Pinpoint The Bug

"The horseshoe was lost for want of a nail..."

- (anonymous) nursery rhyme

Talking about what went wrong... do you know why you made that mistake? When you don't know why it happened, you will not learn much about your mistakes. When things go wrong, because what happened is not obvious to you, backtrack down the road that led you to the mistake and finds out where you were straying.

In his book Welcoming Disaster: Tales from the Brink of Technology, James R. Chiles tells the sordid story of a North Sea floating dormitory designed for offshore oil workers. The dormitory rolled over in the water for one night, killing more than a hundred people. The architects responsible for constructing the dormitory ran to find an excuse and finally found that the sequence of events leading to the tragedy was responsible for one minor fracture in the support system, which had been painted over rather than adequately fixed.

You would be able to prevent future disasters by finding the root of your errors. Take accountability for properly investigating the errors, so you can prevent the ripple impact that one minor error can have.

Tell about it

While you don't have to admit your faults, talking about your issues with a sympathetic ear is often useful especially if that ear belongs to a person who knows more about the target you're trying to accomplish.

There is nothing wrong with asking for help if you're having trouble getting through anything. Seek out a professional or someone you know who has had the same experience you have, tell them what you think you're doing wrong, and listen to what they have to say. The most precious guidance we get always arrives from unexpected outlets, so don't hesitate to ask anyone else about it.

The Power of Positive Investment in Yourself

Unable to locate an expert? The easy act of chatting about your problems to a friend or loved one can be the catalyst you need to keep going through your mistakes. When you address what you've been missing aloud, you may be able to figure out just what you need to alter with your approach; or you may only end up feeling calm, refreshed, and eager to tackle the topic again.

Keep fine records

When you make them, mistakes will not sound very funny to you but someday you will be able to look back and laugh. Even you will be able to look back and remember. You will have a solid plan you will pursue over and over again to achieve your milestones by keeping a comprehensive record of your success, errors, and everything.

A sample error log is given below. As long as you know how to read it, you can use this format, or make your own!

You will find rapid development in your mental garden as you pursue the method of learning from your errors. Mistakes are a fact of life; we will have no discovery without them—and not anything to laugh at.

Add More Fertilizer if Your Buds Shrivel

"Seven times to fall, eight to stand up."

-Proverb of Japanese

Like any method, as you begin to backslide, there will come a period in your attempt to unlock the power of positive thought. You can be tempted to avoid using positive thinking entirely if the condition becomes extraordinarily complicated. This is completely the worst thing you can do though.

"One step beyond what looked like their biggest failure, most individuals achieve their greatest achievements."

— Brian Tracy

Hang out there! Know that to make them, the more improvements you decide to make in your life, the harder you will have to focus on positive thoughts. It is starting to get better. If you like you're beginning to lose ground, the only thing you can do is to keep thinking positively. To assist you through the tough patches, this segment will cover stuff to hold in mind.

The Power of Positive Investment in Yourself

Go Out through the Window if the Door Shuts

It's about fulfilling the milestones you've set for yourself. You could be pursuing your ambitions in the wrong direction if you constantly come up against challenges that appear insurmountable. For any dilemma, there's always a solution; it just may not be what you expected.

Move back from the condition to the big picture and continue to look at it. Are you running yourself against a brick wall repeatedly? If so, maybe you should try walking around or jumping over it instead of attempting to smash through the resistance.

One instance may be trying to move jobs. Have you put your resume in at any organization available, only to be turned down or told that there were no vacancies open? You may think of your profession as a whole in this situation.

Are you still happy with doing what you do? If you are in other sectors you might look at, maybe there is related work. If not, you might want to consider leaving a different company's quest for the same job and begin grooming yourself for a whole new profession. It's never too late to continue doing what you enjoy, and you might be persuaded by those brick walls that the direction you're trying to take isn't right for you.

The Power of Positive Investment in Yourself

When the mountain crumbles, Crushed Alive: What to Do

Tragedy at any moment will hit any one of us. Life is fragile and volatile, and a dramatic shift in life can be caused by any number of events. The most well-laid plans can be devastated by company cuts, a drastic and unpredictable change, a crippling injury, or the death of a loved one.

The first thing you can do is find some time off yourself after a big trauma happens in your life when you are struggling to get things together. You will end up burying feelings that will come back and haunt you if you decide to keep going as if all is perfect and nothing has changed. Buried suffering will as efficiently poison your mental garden as arsenic-laced groundwater. It is important to mourn severe losses in life correctly, if only so that you can truly appreciate what is lost and learn to prepare for it.

Review the stressful experience using the prism of positive thinking after ample time has elapsed to allow you to interpret the situation with greater objectivity. What was the bright side of the scenario? Have there been any things to learn from it? How has the incident changed you, and can you become a better, more positive person by leveraging the change?

The Power of Positive Investment in Yourself

A significant phase in your ability to persevere through difficult times is to face disaster as it happens. You don't have to hide from tragedy—but you don't have to let your soul crush you and drain your life, either. When they arise, lament the defeats, but build the capacity to discern when it's time to move on.

Your Lifelines Use

Have you got a network of support? It is nice to have friends and family you can talk to and share your problems with when your positive thoughts tend to slip down your path to success. Hearing words of affirmation, especially from people who know what you're trying to do will give you the impetus you need to keep moving, even though you don't see the light at the end of a curve in your tunnel.

You should also be able to call on yourself and your own energy reserves to take you through hard times. When you have made a deal with yourself to accomplish a certain purpose, go back, and study it. Have you kept to your initial intentions or moved away from your plan for success? The opportunity to go back to find out where you have driven astray, and retrace your steps so you can stick to your intentions is one benefit to making a comprehensive strategy to accomplish your goals.

Have you kept your journal with you? Try looking back and focusing on what you have done so far if you continue to lose confidence in the power of positive thinking. Even if things are complicated for you right now, you should have already proved to yourself that being a bundle of garbage works reasonably well for constructive thinking. When your first harvest does not make it all the way, don't be afraid to pile on a fresh load of fertilizer.

You should soon be well on your way to the harvest, which is the discovery of what you want out of life because you've had a few false starts or found your natural green thumb. Your tender shoots will grow into solid plants; life continues to send your way capable of weathering the toughest storms. The first blossoms of your efforts are about to be seen, popping like daisies in the spring from the melting crust of your former self.

The Power of Positive Investment in Yourself

OPENING YOUR BLOSSOMS

"Opportunity seldom knocks on the home. Knock quite on opportunity's

door if you ardently want to enter."

- Charles Forbes

You will begin to see the buds of opportunity emerging everywhere in

your life now that your current optimistic outlook is deeply planted in

your mental greenhouse. You should benefit from the infinite fertile fields

around you to coax blossoming success. An important part of reaching

your goals is understanding chance; whether it is delicate as clover or

dazzling as a sunflower.

We will discuss tips and strategies for understanding the full extent of the

influence of positive thought in this segment.

Poppy Fields: In Technicolor, Visualizing

We have to be over the rainbow!"

- In The Wizard of Oz, Dorothy Gale

The Power of Positive Investment in Yourself

The enchanted moment when Judy Garland's Dorothy walks out of the ruins of her black-and-white house into a breathtakingly vibrant universe is remembered by everyone who has seen the timeless classic film The Wizard of Oz, a world she later learned had been there all along. It is like capturing the movie magic for yourself to know the power of positive thought. Suddenly, in a whole new way, your surroundings appear: alive with your life's possibilities and ripe for picking.

Visualization is one important way to obtain access to positive thinking. This implies imagining yourself truly fulfilling your goals and being the person you wish to be. Using visualization may feel uncomfortable at first, like many of the processes we have discussed so far. Solo practice is the perfect way to start using visualization, but finally, in some situations, you will be able to begin the visualization process in just about any case.

The most important thing about visualization that you can learn is this: it only works if you truly, really want it to work. You have to be completely sure of your idea, whatever you envision, whether it's a material target or a new mental mindset. This approach is focused on mental energy because the bigger the theories are the more likely they are to affect your life.

Preparation: Boarding the Train for Simulation

There are various types of methods of visualization, but the first step is still the same in every one of them. To be able to completely immerse your mind, you must emotionally brace yourself to obtain your vision. The method of planning for visualization is much the same as meditation, except as you acquire more familiarity with the process, you will bring in your components.

- Find an undisturbed, peaceful place. Initially, as you imagine, you may need to be alone. Choose a room or area that you can use during the beginning phases for simulation on an exclusive basis. Make sure that the room is calm and uninterrupted. White noise is suitable for simulation, but you do not use music or captured sound for other approaches (you can show your sounds!).
- Get yourself happy. From a sitting role, the easiest way to do visualization is. As long as you sit down in a way that will allow you to stay comfortably for at least ten to fifteen minutes, you can use a comfortable chair or the floor or floor.

- Set a timer. The results of visualization differ from person to person, but it may trigger a trance-like state in certain situations. Get a quiet electronic timer (no ticking!) or set an alarm clock to go off in fifteen to twenty minutes to ensure you don't end up visualizing the day away (at this stage, you still have a few minutes of planning before you begin the visualization process). Calm the body. If you happen to have the potential to rest at will, do that! You should indulge in incremental stimulation to drain the stress from your muscles if you are like most of us and you do not. Start at your feet and focus, one body part at a time, on removing all stress. It will take you a couple of tries to do this; don't panic if the first try doesn't happen. Total recovery will be difficult to obtain, as there may be some stress or stiffness left in certain situations. You will note that the more relaxation you practice more frequently; the less anxiety remains.

- Empty your mind. There are a couple of ways to do this you can pick the one that fits best for you. One approach is to visualize a single, innocuous thing, such as a white ball or a leaf, and before all the other thoughts simmer down, concentrate solely on the imagined object. Image your feelings, with the object in the middle, as an audience in a football stadium. When the mind is drawn to the object, each thought stills until they are all quiet. To "send" your emotions away by covering them in a mental "bubble" and encouraging them to float away from your consciousness is another way to clear your mind.

- Breathe. You can do three to five minutes of slow, intense breathing after you have relaxed your body and cleared your mind. Try to remain concentrating on nothing except your breathing; this will help calm you and prepare your mind to undergo visualization.

As an alternative method of meditation, you can also use this guide to visualization. It is often helpful to take a few minutes to rest, and it will energize you to tackle the challenges you have planned for yourself.

You should select the sort of visualization you want to use to make yourself aware of the process involved before you begin your planning activities. Then you will be able to go straight to visualization from training.

The Power of Positive Investment in Yourself

Guided visualization

Perhaps the most effective method possible is directed visualization. You serve as the captain of your imaginative ship in this process, directing yourself through the visions you conceive as though they were occurring. It is highly important to set your timer when using directed visualization, as it is possible to get wrapped up in your visualized reality.

You need to do a bit of planning to execute guided visualization. Choose an environment or scenario where you feel relaxed and securely bind the setting to your mind: a sandy beach, a dense jungle, or even an open-air mall (if you feel happier away from nature and prefer to see lots of bugs).

For focusing on your feelings and attitudes, driven visualization is the easiest. Decide if it's getting more optimistic, losing weight, or just feeling comfortable and at ease before you begin the way you want to imagine yourself. Tell yourself that the location you go will give you the strength to fulfill certain thoughts, feelings, or features. Don't imagine watching yourself perform the desired acts when you begin your simulation after your planning process. Alternatively, try to feel as if you are really doing them: as if you have unexpectedly shed fifty pounds, or earned a strong dose of faith. Maybe you would even like to let yourself ride! (Just make sure that, whether it's boarding a plane, you're not trying to transform your newfound flight abilities into actual life experience).

With the help of audio software or themed songs, you may also execute guided simulation. The first several times, you will want to try guided meditation tapes, and then step away from them steadily before you can execute this process on your own. After all, it is your subconscious that you are attempting to reprogram and to accomplish your personal goals, you can fill it with your ideas, perceptions, and emotions.

Receptive visualization

Receptive visualization is another method of visualization. This differs from the directed simulation in that instead of doing something, you are seeing yourself. For working on experiences with other individuals, receptive visualization is a successful strategy. For starters, you can imagine yourself doing it flawlessly and convincingly if you want to ask someone out on a date, and then visualize your goal by accepting.

Doing responsive simulation, with you as the director, is almost like watching a movie in your mind. The benefit of responsive visualization is that a single idea will modify anything as things tend to go in a different direction than the way you expect them. You are in total charge, and the more you imagine a scenario absolutely and always, the more likely it would be to arise exactly the way you imagined it.

You can use it just about anywhere in any situation since you've mastered receptive visualization. Imagine, for instance, that you go to the bank to make a withdrawal, but you find that there is an issue with your account before you hit the teller and you have to talk to a bank manager. You should imagine your discussion with the boss as you're waiting, and emotionally settle the matter in your favor. Then you will be able to face the situation confidently and with confidence when you finally talk to the boss.

Things are going to progress vary according to your view, more frequently than not.

The most useful visualization approach for daily activities is receptive visualization. Since it is flexible and adaptable, you can address virtually any issue using receptive visualization. You will be able to go through your day with a sense of trust that it will work out exactly as you want it to, and other people will react to you in a friendly way because of your projected

The Power of Positive Investment in Yourself

confidence. It can relieve the pressures of everyday life by exercising your receptive visualization skills, which in turn enhances the entire condition.

Visualization of Altered Memories

Altered memory visualization is the next visualization method we will explore. In settling past disputes and soothing frustration, this form is particularly useful. You may either be" the picture in altered memory visualization or watch yourself, whichever you are more relaxed with. The primary aim of the simulation of altered memory is to visualize a real memory and adjust the effect in your head to create a different, more satisfactory resolution.

For minor problems like being cut off in traffic or wider fields such as past disaster or pain, you may use altered memory visualization. Again with this procedure, especially when dealing with major traumas, it is necessary to use a timer. It's so easy to get so lost in your memories that it's not possible to shake them.

Start recalling the incident where you intend to change the way it happened, whether you want to watch or join. Try to remember, exactly as they were, all the sights, sounds, and smells. Guide yourself to react differently from the way you did, or direct the other party to do something else when you hit an awkward point in your memory. You will be able to transfer your mental images to a more optimistic sequence of events easily with practice, and the emotions you previously associated with your memories will fade in their effects on you. An important tool for forgiveness, whether you aim it towards yourself or anyone else is using altered memory animation.

You can improve and increase the positive thinking base by using simulation strategies and exercising regularly. The first step to fulfilling them is to imagine your wishes. You can do whatever you think you can and visualization can help you achieve your goals more easily and with less effort.

Concern-Me-Nots and You-Can-Themums

"Those who win sooner or later are those who think they can."

—Richard Bach

Believing in yourself and your talents are the most important thing on your road to positive thinking that you can do. To build the self-

The Power of Positive Investment in Yourself

confidence you need to take you forward to the accomplishment of your objectives is important.

A little bit different from self-esteem is self-confidence. Self-esteem refers to your thoughts as a human about yourself, your actions, and your worth. Your pride in your ability and in the way you show yourself to the world is self-confidence. Others' acts are more likely to erode your trust in yourself rather than your self-esteem. The two feelings have quite a deal in common, though. Both are metrics of your innate or proven self-belief, and both can easily be forced off-balance, leading to over-confident or defeatist habits that separate you from your ultimate goals.

You need to build a compromise between too little self-confidence and too much, as previously mentioned. Without self-confidence, you can't do anything, on the other hand, too much self-confidence can ensure you're not working hard enough to attain your ambitions, and you're going to fall short of understanding the possibilities.

You would have opened the secret to a good thought until you realize that you can do anything you set your mind to. There is no limit to the human mind's power. Your options are limitless.

The Power of Positive Investment in Yourself

After understanding the fundamental principle, you can help yourself gain

self-confidence with a basic everyday exercise that you develop yourself.

You can feel silly at first, like any of the practices for dealing with positive

thinking (yes, we are trying to make you feel ridiculous. We bust out the

flowered hats and funny nose glasses next). Here are the foundational

steps to the everyday regimen of self-confidence, which is better carried

out in the morning while you plan to face the day:

- Decimate distractions. You need yourself this time. This time, you

  deserve to be yourself. Don't answer the phone, read your e-mail,

  watch TV, or listen to the radio as you practice your self-

  confidence routine. Let the members of the family know that this

  moment is your time and you'd rather not be bothered.

- Get physical. In your daily physical preparations, pamper yourself.

  Use your favorite soap or scented body wash while you shower.

  Choose clothes that make you feel comfortable and conform to

  your mood. With the way you pose, make yourself happy, and

  your self-confidence will grow to fit it.

- Forward emphasis. Reflect on what you want to do for the day

  when you get dressed. Make sure to understand both the mood

  you intend to create for yourself and any ambitions or goals you're going to achieve. To visualize yourself achieving your targets and cement them in your head, you might also engage in a short responsive visualization session.

- Pump

- Get pumped. The ridiculous part comes now. Stand in front of a mirror, look at your eyes, and sing praises of your own. Loud out. Tell yourself that you are the person you aspire to be; that you have worthy qualities; that you should do what you are going to do now. Be as concrete as possible. Instead of saying, "I am competent," say: "When they arise, I know how to handle problems." The more precise you are the more successful your routine of self-confidence can prove to be.

The glue that keeps your identity intact is self-confidence. Developing positive self-confidence will prepare you to do it easily and effortlessly if you are serious about transforming your life. Do not let terror, anxiety, and uncertainty prevent you from blossoming into faith. As long as you know you can, you can do something. It's truly as plain as that.

Cross-Pollination: The "Bee" How To

The Power of Positive Investment in Yourself

"We regulate our lives by our attitudes. Attitudes are a hidden force that works twenty-four hours a day for better or for worse. It is of utmost importance that we know how to manipulate this great power and regulate it.

- Tom Blandi, Tom Blandi

The way you believe it is perhaps as critical as what you believe. A miserable occurrence will turn your mood into a fun one or a nice time into a nightmare. You can manipulate any situation and build what you expect from it by managing your mindset.

You should take some time to consider the type of individual you want to be and the picture you want to portray, to evaluate the right mindset for any given situation. With the opportunity to take the lead at any time, you might be interested in being the life of the party, the quintessential sympathetic ear, or the powerful and silent sort. You will continue to change your personality to match until you are conscious of your true self.

When you build your attitude habits, here are a few essential factors to bear in mind:

That Bee Yourself

The Power of Positive Investment in Yourself

"He who trims himself to suit everybody is going to whittle himself away soon."

—Raymond Hull

Make sure it is a representation of your true self, whichever mentality you want. For the effectiveness of your positive thinking program, being true to oneself is important. You just have one life to live, and spending it trying to imitate someone else is robbing the world of the person you would have become.

You do not know yourself as well as you like to, or as well as you ought to know. You may have learned more than you know before if you have been using the approaches in this book so far. One of humanity's most beautiful qualities is that there is always something new to learn about ourselves; there is always a fresh avenue of concern to discover or stand to take. We have the opportunity never to succumb to boredom. Incredibly, so many people feel lulls with all the action going on in the world and do not find something to concern themselves with. If you ever get bored, you have finished developing as an entity and can take action to quickly rectify the situation. It is a continuous quest to know yourself and should never end.

The Power of Positive Investment in Yourself

How do you get well acquainted with yourself? To uncover facets of your personality that you might not otherwise have known existed, try any of the following techniques:

- Date Yourself. Choose an activity that you either know you like or think you're going to enjoy and make a date for yourself to do it. Treat this date as any other engagement you would like: dress nicely, be on schedule, and don't put it off unless there is an absolute emergency. Remember the stuff that makes you feel comfortable when you walk out on your date. Enjoy the feeling of doing something enjoyable and being by yourself. When you are done, much as you will in every other case, focus on the date. What did you like about this experience? What have you disliked? What will you change? Even if it's just for a walk in the woods or an evening on the couch with popcorn and rented movies, you can have a date with yourself at least once a month.

- Conversation with Yourself. You are eager to speak to other people intelligently to find out more about them. Why not just do the same for yourself? Aloud or in your mind, you should have a conversation with yourself, however, you feel comfortable with. Tell yourself the leading questions, and then take some time for truthful responses to be considered. The biggest crime you can do is lying to yourself.

- Recording Yourself. Write them down and recall them as you find new facets of your personality or sparks of curiosity that you didn't know you had. You do not have time to discuss a single idea when it comes to you, so you may be able to expound on it if you jot it down and come back to it later. Holding a little diary or planner with you to write stuff down when they happen to you can be useful, then flip through it anytime you have a couple of spare minutes.

- Analyzing Yourself. It can be very revealing about the way you respond to social circumstances and world events. Keep yourself updated on what's going on in the country, either by reading the newspaper, watching TV news, or visiting blogs with news feeds. Take note of your responses to actual events and scenarios, and strive to adapt them in your life to situations. You will use this to help you decide why you feel towards individuals or things that shape your daily life in a particular way, and then organize your behavior about them around your newfound awareness.

Bee happy bee

The Power of Positive Investment in Yourself

"Happiness is not something for the future that you postpone; it is something for the present that you design."

—Jim Rohn

Maybe you're one of those people right now saying, "You can't tell me to be happy." If I don't want to, I don't have to be happy. Shouldn't this help me discover my real self? What if I'm just not a happy person? Think of this if you are one of those people: not being happy makes you happy.

Now, aren't you happy?

"Happy" is a highly intangible emotion. It won't always satisfy anyone else what makes one person happy. You must describe your satisfaction, and aspire wherever possible to attain that condition.

Happiness is infectious as well. A little bit of pleasure goes a long way, which has a snowball effect—because it makes others around you happier when you are happy; so they extend the happiness to everyone in exchange. A major part of generating a consistently optimistic outlook is seeking satisfaction with everything you do.

The Power of Positive Investment in Yourself

It is a waste of time to do stuff that ultimately won't make you happy. Set your mood to "happy" will guarantee that the job is completed with minimum tension and optimum performance when you are faced with an unpleasant task that must nonetheless be accomplished. Alternatively, if you have the option to do something and you know it would not make you happier, practice the right to improve by saying "no If you chose not to want it to, nothing will make you miserable. The strength of positive thinking is this.

A happy discovery. Need any assistance in finding your happy spring? Test a couple of these cheerful tapping approaches:

- Act like an infant. Children are the happiest beings on Earth in general. A perfect way to create a sense of the carefree fun you experienced is to participate in the things you cherished as a child. Only for the fun of running, do somersaults or jumping jacks, or spin in place before you get so dizzy you fall over. Blast bubbles, swing as far as you can, sprint around the grass. For the spirit, a daily dose of childlike joy is a soothing balm. Uninhibited be!

The Power of Positive Investment in Yourself

- Constructing a treasure box. Pleasant staff reminders will be a great jumpstart to the stores of pleasure. If you have little vacation tokens that you liked, sweet letters from friends or loved ones, or important things that you picked up here and there "just because," consider making a box to store them in so that you can go through it whenever you notice the blues attack coming on. Anything that catches your favorite smells will be a perfect addition to your treasure chest. The scent is the strongest sensory stimulus there is, and it will raise your spirits much more powerfully than anything else by being able to perceive a fragrance with good connotations.

- Enjoy the little things. It's not easy to underestimate the value of small things that make you smile. A favorite novel, the sound of the laughter of your kids, the smell of fresh popcorn or moist soil after the rain; to create enjoyment, you should access all of the hundred little things you find delight in. Keep a mental list of your favorite little stuff and draw on it if you feel content for a few quarts.

- Chuckle. Laugh, just. You're not going to need a cause or even a trigger. Just start laughing at any given moment, no matter where you are or what you are doing. Laughter would give you an instant

mood lift that lasts for long periods and increases your

commitment to be happy.

Bee-have

Trust males and they are going to be accurate to you; handle them

considerably, and they'll teach themselves excellently.

- Ralph Waldo Emerson

A representation of your personality is the way you handle other people.

You should not expect a good outlook to be maintained when behaving

aggressively towards others. You have to try to maintain a sense of pride

and enthusiasm even though the good spirit is not restored. Ultimately,

those who grudge your satisfaction will either give in and join you or give

up and go away-and in either case, without bowing to negativity yourself,

you will be free of the detrimental effect.

How do you refrain from poorly treating other individuals? Your conduct

lies in the answer. When coping with negative thoughts from others, it is

not so much what you should do as what you should not do. Such basic

tips for behaving better and maintaining your good outlook are as follows:

DON'T throw fits. When they don't get their way, several persons succumb to temper tantrums. Without even understanding it others do this. Ranting over the unfairness of the situation will not change things; creating angrier feelings and feeding the fire is what it will do. You certainly won't give in to the person you're facing because you're complaining. When you begin to have a meltdown, learn to recognize the symptoms, and allow yourself to stand back and take a more logical look at the situation. Perhaps there is more to it than you first noticed.

DON'T stay mad. It is appropriate to get mad, and even helpful in certain situations. An effective driving force maybe rage. Getting mad, though, is much different from remaining angry. It is futile to hold on to your rage; you will stay where you are in the scenario and nothing will change but the level of your anger. Take your frustration and turn its energies into doing something about the situation when someone or something makes you angry. Using your anger to do something for yourself if there is little to be done. But whatever you're doing, don't let rage trap you stuck in the place.

DON'T hold grudges. For as long as they live, nearly everyone will think about at least one person they have promised never to speak to again. You may be able to think of some persons that fell under this group. It can happen naturally to hold a grudge against someone, or it may be a deliberately orchestrated and conducted attack. Some individuals have raised grudge-holding to an art form, causing everyone else around them to take special care for family reunion seating arrangements to prevent bringing together individuals who ignore each other loudly. It's quick to form a grudge, and it's infinitely more difficult to let one go. To keep a good outlook, though, you must let go of grudges. When you are reminded of the person you are not referring to, sustaining depressive thoughts over a prolonged period can taint your emotional garden, and provide an automatic supply of negativity. You are expending energies that might otherwise be used to enrich your own life by nursing a grudge. If you choose not to chat with someone you're upset with, that's a decision you should make. The easiest solution is to agree to disagree and go your separate ways. Letting go makes you, inside and out, a happier person.

DON'T Behave Superior. Believing that you are better than others, even though it's the truth, is a harmful mindset. A little bit of modesty goes a long way. You will find your confidence growing and your mood improving as people are relaxed communicating with you. It is a risky proposition to bring someone else down to make yourself feel better, and it will backfire and come to haunt you more frequently than not. Be the best person you can be, but do not make yourself feel superior to yourself. In the end, we are all merely people.

DO for Others. The safest rule to obey is always the Golden Rule. Treat other persons the way you wish to be handled, and they will follow your lead finally. It will still come back to you in one shape or another when you show courtesy and generosity to others, even when you least anticipate it. It is possible to forgive and forget angry words and hurtful acts, but good deeds endure for a lifetime. And if you are not given the same by the people you regard with respect, take comfort in the fact that you are behaving with honesty and have nothing to be ashamed of. A lack of remorse breeds fearlessness and anything can be done for courageous people.

Bee flexible

If we paid attention to the intellect of ours, we would certainly not have a love affair. We would certainly not have a friendship. We would certainly not go into business, since we would be way too skeptical. Effectively,

The Power of Positive Investment in Yourself

that is nonsense. You have got to jump off cliffs all of the time and grow

the wings on how down.

- Ray Bradbury

You must be able to bend and ready to pursue a new direction to

positivism as life impacts your mentality. It is analogous to standing in the

middle of a storm to live an inflexible life. You will be swept away no

matter what you want to hang on to and your dreams will be altered for

you. You must be able to change your habits and laws and encourage life

to take you to the places you want to go to.

If we expect to evolve as a human, we must be able to adjust to our

circumstances. Eminent evolutionist Charles Darwin once said It is not the

strongest or most intelligent of the surviving species, but those most

adaptable to change." Inflexible systems are more vulnerable to cracking,

no matter how solidly they are made. You must learn to give and bend.

Flexibility also helps you to explore new possibilities that you would have

overlooked otherwise. You could still drive the same route to work, for

example. What would you do, though if the morning traffic report on your

regular route showed congestion? You have a choice: for an extended amount of time, you can either follow the same direction you usually take and wait in traffic, or you can pick an alternative route. You could discover a new restaurant you didn't know was around, or see the sunrise over a whole new world if you chose an alternative path.

To improve your versatility and train yourself to be open to transition, there are steps you should take. Here are a few suggestions to preserve versatility and to be prepared to take advantage of new possibilities when they arise:

- Giving time to yourself. Be sure you have more than enough time to make it if you are making a meeting or trying to go anywhere. Try to keep a gap open: permit yourself to say "I'll be there between 7 and 8" rather than saying "I'll be there at 7:30."

- Formulate Plan B. In the event of anything going wrong, please have a contingency plan available. This way, in the absence of your initial plans, you are not left unaware and can have more of a sense of what you should do. When you already have options in mind, it is better to be versatile.

- Do something new. Try tossing in a few changes if there are certain routines you adopt with certain things. For starters, if you ride public transit to work and still sit in the same section of the train or bus, decide for a few trips to sit elsewhere. You may discover something that you haven't seen before or you might have the chance to meet new people.

- Spontaneous Being. Whenever possible, do something that you wouldn't necessarily do. Spontaneity is a perfect way to build variety, so you don't know what to expect on your own, because you're going to be pushed to make up for your lack of preparation. Often practice improvisation, and quest for innovative alternatives to traditional concerns. Different is fine, particularly if it helps you to improve your adaptive versatility and capacity.

Your mentality dictates your result. You will build your satisfaction as you develop the ability to control your mood. Without the mindset, nothing exists, because the way you feel about something you do will influence the way it is done.

If you can't build an optimistic outlook right away, you may only "fake it until you make it to persuade yourself of your excitement, use the power of positive thoughts, and then you may finally begin to feel confident about whatever it is you're striving to achieve. Life is what you make of it and your life is your mindset. Tend well to it.

FRUITION AND HARVEST

There's far more to us than we know. If perhaps we can be made seeing it, maybe for the majority of the lives of ours we are going to be reluctant to settle for a cheaper price.

- Kurt Hahn

Truly amazing are the advantages of positive thinking. They will expand to any part of your life, and you will feel like an entirely new entity. The strength of positive thinking is the strength of change. When you think positively, it's not just inside yourself that the changes happen. When you radiate optimism and good feelings, the rest of the world will respond to your new perspective. Not only can you become a happier individual, but you will also be a better person to be around.

The most exciting part of your journey through positive thinking is harvesting the fruits of your work. We will explore in this chapter the various advantages you can hope to achieve from applying positive thinking to all facets of your life. When you follow the strategies previously mentioned, you will find that positive things only tend to happen to you. You're going to become the lucky guy you've always envied, the one that appears to be a magnet for luck and love.

Natural Attraction: Bringing Love, Success as well as Money

People who bring sunshine into the lives of others, can't keep it from themselves.

- Sir James M. Barrie

A whole new world of possibility is opened by the influence of positive thinking. You will discover the benefits of sustaining a constructive mindset, such as water drained by a sponge, seeping into all aspects of your life. When your newfound perspective and behavior infect your mind, your surroundings, and your family and friends with pleasure and bring you prosperity beyond your wildest expectations, little will remain unchanged.

Here are only a handful of the many improvements that constructive thinking can bring to your life.

The Radiant Ties

The Power of Positive Investment in Yourself

Relationships, including our relationships with others and with ourselves, are important to our humanity. Our partnerships describe and accentuate who we are, and the way we relate to ourselves is directly related to our willingness to relate to others. In our relationships, the use of constructive reinforcement helps one to enjoy them to the fullest potential and become filled with caring and compassion.

Positive thinking extends our partnerships, enhances, and reinforces them. It also encourages us to build new relationships and enjoy the rewards of communicating with others without causing our lives to be polluted by negativity. Any of the ways that marriages benefit from constructive thinking are:

- Increased confidence: With positive thought, the propensity to lie to yourself is one of the negative habits you can ignore. This would quell the urge to lie to others immediately. You earn trust in return when you put forward trust; when you trust yourself, those who care for you will also place their trust in you.

- Fewer claims: As you advance in positive thinking, you can find that your arguments diminish in both frequency and strength. Generally, this is because you will not be troubled by too many things, and you will be able to practice forgiving more often. If you often fight with your partner, your kids, other family members, or close friends, while you exercise constructive thinking, look forward to a sharp decline in shouting.

- Improved communication: You will be able to express your goals more thoroughly as you understand yourself, your expectations, and your priorities. This would lead to stronger contact, which is the secret to any partnership that is good. You would automatically inspire people to be honest and clear-thinking too by simply expressing what you are trying to get across. You may even be shocked by your new ability to explain your thoughts and motives!

- More comprehension: This advantage builds on better coordination. It would be easier to convince people of your point of view if you can justify why you agree or disagree with a particular topic, or at least let them understand why you are entitled to your views. In a friendship, empathy facilitates closer bonds and less tension and helps all sides of the equation to relax.

- Better sex: Really, yeah. All the feelings, like physical enjoyment, are awakened by the application of positive thinking. It will improve your sex life by applying positive thinking to your relationships, in part because you can feel—and thus be—more desirable. Beauty truly emerges from inside, and you would be more beautiful than a swimsuit model with the transformative influence of positive thought.

- Stronger bonds: Optimistic thought takes society closer to you. You will grow a strong sense of empathy that will encourage you to see things, including other people's eyes, from alternative points of view. Not only does empathy encourage you to forgive errors; it also allows you a stronger friend and confidante: the kind of person everybody wants to be around. Soon you can figure out that there's plenty of you to go around with.

- Less stress: It can take a toll on us in relationships. Holding relationships intact is always such a strain; you must devote time and energy to nurturing and sustaining each one of them. The strength of positive thought, though, not only frees you from unburdening yourself with dysfunctional relationships; it also helps you to be yourself in all conditions, which decreases the usual tension of partnerships that most of us encounter.

Amazing Careers

The Power of Positive Investment in Yourself

Work isn't a male's punishment. It's the reward of his as well as the strength of his as well as the pleasure of his.

- George Sand

You will assume that most people do not love their work if you accept what the rest of us do. The reality, though, is that many individuals do; they have only forgotten. With hope and expectation, many people begin a career, only to find down the road that their aspirations have been shattered by corporate laws.

Good thought helps you, whether you are a housewife or a CEO, to wring satisfaction from your profession. To rediscover the reason, you joined your chosen profession in the first place is an easy matter, and then to increase certain factors in your everyday working life.

In comparison, many individuals who want to search for the influence of constructive thinking figure out that the profession they have is not the career they desire, no matter how much silver lining they drape around their clouds. Once again to raise you and ease you into your place in the world, constructive thinking moves in.

The Power of Positive Investment in Yourself

Here are only a couple of the ways your job will benefit from constructive thinking:

- Recognition: You become more vivid and alive than you have ever been when you practice constructive thinking. You will find that your contributions are more frequently appreciated and rewarded, particularly when you don't expect acknowledgment. You can stand out clearly by doing your work with a good outlook to the best of your ability.

- Promotions and Raises: In the workplace, people with can-do behaviors advance even quicker. Using the power of positive thought improves your confidence and reveals your capacity to bear more responsibility, and you will be heard and handled appropriately by people above you at work. Not only will you be granted more opportunities; instead of only waiting for the day to end so you can return to your "real life, you can find yourself finding change and satisfaction.

- Better working environment: You can remember the contagiousness of optimistic thoughts. Acting with a friendly attitude can reinforce, or at least the impressions of the attitudes of those around you. When you gain satisfaction from your successes and appreciate the company of your co-workers, you will start to find that your workday no longer drags you down.

- Less Supervision: Most of us know what it's like to breathe down our throats with a boss. When we switch to a constructive mentality, we explain our skills without undue direction (or interference) to complete work satisfactorily. We will do even better left to our own devices, and this will become clear to even the most anal bosses.

- Dream Job: You will live your dreams with optimistic thoughts. You will soon find your profession providing everything you imagine it to be, whether you want to pursue a new path or turn the role you have into the position you enjoy.

- Entrepreneurship: Most individuals long to go into business for themselves but most dread the repercussions of risking someone else's safety and security. Positive thought frees you from your fear of change and equips you with the resources you need to not only take action to succeed for yourself but to add success to your entrepreneurial vision. You should use optimistic thinking to bypass the traps that haunt most early entrepreneurial ventures and realize your hopes of self-employment, whatever the motives

for wanting your own business.

- Different possibilities: Optimistic thought helps you to imagine

  chances that you would otherwise have overlooked. You'll better

  understand what you're looking for in a profession when you get

  to know yourself, your values, and your aspirations. You will also

  be able to find the means to do what you want, whether it's

  improving your present work, receiving a promotion or new role,

  or going off on your own. With the power of positive thinking,

  there is no end to the possibilities awaiting you.

This is not to suggest that you would be wealthy from positive thinking,

although that is a clear probability. Achieving financial freedom is freeing

yourself from the stresses that money brings and enabling yourself, if not

a surplus, to still have plenty.

Any of the aspects that financial freedom is promoted by optimistic

thinking:

- Infinite options. If you want to be wealthy and debt-free or live in

  an ocean-side house, when you know that every path is available to you, you will take steps to set and accomplish your financial targets.

- Positive working climate. Since optimistic thinking equips you with the opportunity to love your work, you will find yourself doing even more and gaining more naturally, whether it be in the form of raises, promotions, or the decision that somewhere else you are better off.

- The lower outflow of cash. You will find yourself wasting less money as you practice constructive thinking strategies. There will be fewer emergencies and tragedies in your life when you are responsible and trustworthy, and tragedy will become a rare occurrence; a simple recollection. One of the main long-term advantages of positive thinking is investing less to earn more. To fulfill yourself as you grow wealthier in spirit, you can also find that you need less material things.

Economic Freedom

"If an individual gets the attitude of his toward cash directly, it'll help straighten out nearly every other area in his life."

- Billy Graham

The Power of Positive Investment in Yourself

This is not to suggest that you would be wealthy from positive thinking, although that is a clear probability. Achieving financial freedom is freeing yourself from the stresses that money brings and enabling yourself, if not a surplus, to still have plenty.

Any of the aspects that financial freedom is promoted by optimistic thinking:

- Infinite options. If you want to be wealthy and debt-free or live in an ocean-side house, when you know that every path is available to you, you will take steps to set and accomplish your financial targets.

- Positive working climate. Since optimistic thinking equips you with the opportunity to love your work, you will find yourself doing even more and gaining more naturally, whether it be in the form of raises, promotions, or the decision that somewhere else you are better off.

- The lower outflow of cash. You will find yourself wasting less money as you practice constructive thinking strategies. There will be fewer emergencies and tragedies in your life when you are responsible and trustworthy, and tragedy will become a rare occurrence; a simple recollection. One of the main long-term advantages of positive thinking is investing less to earn more. To fulfill yourself as you grow wealthier in spirit, you can also find that you need less material things.

Fantasy Delivery

"If you've built castles of the air, the work need not be lost; there's exactly where they should be. Today put foundations beneath them."

- Henry David Thoreau

Good thought will help you reach them, whatever your goals are about your life. Whether it is traveling to an exotic destination, attempting a daredevil trick, or meeting a specific celebrity, lifelong dreams can take several forms. You should take the required steps of optimistic thoughts to make the fondest wishes a reality.

A target is said to be a dream with a deadline. Positive thinking makes you not only understand that your dreams can be lived, but that you deserve to live them. Good thought encourages you to:

- Understand that no dream is too big or too small.

- Build a mentality that is conducive to achieving wishes.

- Formulate a concrete, manageable roadmap for fulfilling your dreams.

- Equip yourself with the determination required before you hit your dream to keep going.

- Dream greater than you can ever have, remember that there is no end to what you can do.

Outstanding Aging

"Youth is a circumstance you cannot do something about. The trick is growing up without getting old."

- Frank Lloyd Wright

What's so good about aging? When you approach everything through the prism of positive thinking, everything. Studies have found that happier people survive, on average, 7.5 years longer than negative people, a greater benefit than not smoking, eating daily, and keeping a healthier weight together The introduction of constructive reinforcement strategies to the aging process has an amazing impact.

The Power of Positive Investment in Yourself

You grant yourself the gift of time by encouraging yourself to treat aging as an experience rather than an ordeal. Below are some other advantages of a healthy aging outlook:

- Lowered cholesterol and lowered blood pressure. Happy people don't face a lot of tension. They prefer to keep themselves in better shape as well. The rise in life expectancy for positive individuals is attributed by some studies to the subsequent decline in blood pressure and cholesterol.

- Stronger will for life. All of us seem to lapse into a depressed mood as we age. We always dwell on our lives and conclude that we have not done anything deserving of merit, and so we start to die. We will remember by positive thinking that it is never too late to do more with ourselves and our lives; that there is no lack in anything.

- Preserving freedom. You can note that certain older individuals appear much younger and more capable of their age than others. The biggest difference is mentality between a 70-year-old who lives at home, remains occupied, and keeps an engaged family life; and a 70-year-old who is disabled in a nursing home and consigned to a wheelchair. The senior at home claims that no matter how old they get it is possible to have a safe, prosperous life, whilst the senior at home feels that there is little to look forward to.

THE PHYSICAL POWER OF POSITIVE THINKING

"Take care of the body with steadfast fidelity. The soul should see through these eyes by itself, and if they're dark, the entire earth is clouded."

¬- Goethe

You know that your mental health is strengthened by positive thinking. But did you know that it will improve your physical fitness as well? The control of your emotions is so powerful that it can potentially impact the actions of the body and enhance a host of physical ailments-or even pull you from the verge of death.

Take Reeve from Christopher. Since a horse-riding accident left him crippled, the star who will be long remembered for his strong role as Superman will still be remembered for his amazing recovery. But Reeve not only lasted much longer than any doctor had expected, but he also took great strides in healing and was able to move portions of his body that had been pronounced losing to him permanently until he died in 2004. After the crash, Reeve survived for nine years and proved he was a superhero.

When was he doing that? Looking positively. Reeve's positive outlook and can-do mentality were almost exclusively responsible for the unprecedented degree of healing he achieved, according to experts who studied his event.

Your physical fitness reacts tremendously as you banish unpleasant feelings from your head. It has been understood for a long time that there is a link between mental and physical wellbeing, also referred to as the "connection between mind and body." Changing your mindset and practicing constructive thinking enhances the connection between mind and body and keeps you healthier, even to the point of extending your life.

Studies have found that antibodies are decreased by stress and pessimistic thoughts and leaving you more vulnerable to infection and sickness. Those who are unhappy or stressed exhibit weaker immune responses to vaccines; take longer to heal; are more susceptible to colds and viruses, and experience stronger symptoms.

The Power of Positive Investment in Yourself

There are established scientific evidence that emotion-related electrical activity in the brain has a significant effect on the capacity of the body to recover and battle the disease. Negative thoughts generate an increase in activity in the right prefrontal cortex, resulting in a poor immune response, while positive thinking generates activity in the left prefrontal cortex and enhances the immune response. It is true: happier people are safer, precisely because they are happy!

A motivational outlook program can also have the potential to shield you from Alzheimer's or other diseases with degenerative aging. Because a constant search for self-improvement is part of the positive thought process and helps you to remain mentally healthy when you age, your mind will be in better condition and you will be less vulnerable to degenerative diseases such as Alzheimer's, osteoporosis, and rheumatoid arthritis. To sustain a sharp body, a sharp mind helps.

Concerning your wellbeing, do not underestimate the influence of positive thought. You should think of yourself as being well, and you'll find you have more resources, fewer colds, and more vitality. Any day maybe, medicine will find a way to inject pleasure as a method of battling illness. We would have to be accountable for building our satisfaction before then.

The Power of Positive Investment in Yourself

Take it easy and Relax

"It is some time to break through the barriers which have held you again and held you down for such a quite a while. It's time to reach out and indelibly etch the spot in history."

- Greg Hickman

Are you ready for a new life?

To fulfill the deepest dreams, wishes, and aspirations, constructive thinking arms you with all the instruments you need. You will be prepared to cope with all of the situations in which life confronts you, and receptive to the infinite opportunities that come with real happiness. You can look back and admire the harvest of progress until you've planted and tended your mental greenhouse.

It is important to relax and celebrate your success as you hit the fruition of your positive thought objectives. When you do not take the time to experience the rewards of all the hard work, you would not be inspired to go forward in your life. Many people do not know how to relax, and they want to force themselves to expect that they will finally obtain relief and compensation. This is not the case: you have to take the time to harvest what you have sown in your mental greenhouse by yourself.

The Power of Positive Investment in Yourself

There are some tips below to help you take the true measure of your results and use them for still more meaningful gains:

- Take a day for "me". Take a whole day off yourself after you have achieved a big objective. You won this. Get interested in your favorite activities: reading a nice book, watching a movie, eating at your favorite restaurant. Pamper yourself: have a long bath, buy a decadent treat for yourself, have a professional massage. Refuse on this day to do favors for someone else. Tell people that you enjoy your achievements and rejoice in emotions of happiness. You will feel wonderful because, in your head, you will cement your accomplishments. To your sustained growth, knowledge of your development is integral.

- Share the love. Will you know anyone with common goals and objectives? Take the opportunity to share your successes with someone else you believe is going to benefit from them. Tell them how your targets have been accomplished and share the secrets of your success. Changing your own life creates a powerful sensation, and your rewards are intensified as you use your transition to make others improve as well. For ourselves, pleasure and accomplishment cannot be contained and maintained. Whenever necessary, encourage the propagation of joy, and you will find your efforts coming back to you again and again.

- Count your blessings. The more you achieve, the more you stand to achieve. It will help you improve your good outlook by focusing on the complete understanding of the achievement of your goals. There may be advantages of the successes you have yet to learn. By meeting your targets, what did you gain? Build and regularly add to a mental catalog of all the ways your life is improved by positive thinking. This exercise adds to the arsenal of resources for empowerment and enhances your ability to learn exponentially.

- Retain the lecture. You should have a written account of your accomplishments, much as you have kept a log of your success in the accomplishment of your goals. For your continuous growth, the capacity to focus on transition and the measures that lead to it is critical. In the future, you could find yourself facing a similar challenge, and getting a series of written notes to turn to saves you as though you had never done it before, the emotional challenges of going through the procedure all over again. In comparison, writing down what you have achieved helps you to explore the true significance of what you have done, and what you have acquired over your primary target.

- Start again. In positive thought, the sentiment "quit while you're ahead" has no location. While the fruits of your labor must be celebrated, it is equally important to set new goals; strive for higher expectations. Never stop to evolve and learn. When you have achieved a stage in your life that satisfies your needs and aspirations, you develop new desires and generate more dreams. It is a journey; life is not a destination. Settling for complacency and stopping living is to accomplish perfection. The day when we cease to change, we begin to die.

Unwind! Relax! You won this. After each performance, just don't forget to continue your search for a fulfilling life. To achieve every objective, whether it is organizing your desk or exploring the globe, use constructive thinking. Your goals will be fulfilled and you can start today. The perfect time to launch the road to fulfillment is right now.

The Power of Positive Investment in Yourself

CONCLUSION

"The bad news is time flies. The best part is you are the pilot."

- Michael Altshuler

Season Survival: Keep your garden alive

Now that you have appreciated the harvest of your thriving mental farm, you need to make sure that, year after year, you can manage to grow a new crop. You can not deter the rain from coming, so when it falls, you can choose how you perceive it. The passing of time and its eroding impact cannot be prevented but you can train yourself to know when it is time to replant. You can't lock people out of your garden—but you can choose to invite them in.

Each time, you will learn to weather the tough times with practice and emerge stronger from hibernation. The more positive thinking you use, the greater your emotional power is going to get. You are squarely on the road to getting what you want from life, and the longer you sit, the harder it would be for you to be deterred by something."

He that decides the start of a street chooses the location it leads to. It's the means that establishes the end."

The Power of Positive Investment in Yourself

- Harry Emerson Fosdick

The journey has started. Wherever it concludes is completely your choice.

CHECKLIST FOR THE POSITIVE THINKING PROCESS

Take these steps to tap into the power of positive thinking when you launch a project or participate in self-improvement.

- ❖ Banish the mind's destructive feelings.

- ❖ Decide to achieve that goal.

- ❖ Formulate a series of constructive ideas circling the target.

- ❖ To achieve your target, create a step-by-step plan.

- ❖ Maintain a diary of your reflections and your success.

- ❖ Practice getting yourself out of your way.

- ❖ In the case of failures, be resilient and willing to begin over.

- ❖ Visualize yourself attaining that purpose.

- ❖ Maintain a favorable attitude towards your target.

- ❖ Do not allow others' views to discourage you from your path.

The Power of Positive Investment in Yourself

❖ Engage in regular exercises of self-confidence to keep the target
   fresh.

❖ Be yourself, act, and be pleased.

❖ Recognize when you have met your goal and appreciate your
   results.

❖ Focus on the direction that took you to your target.

❖ For future reference, record your reactions and suggestions.

BIBLIOGRAPHY

Beaulac, Andrew. "Yak Riders on Meditation Methods."

http://www.yakrider.com/meditation_methods.htm, January 2000

Brescia, Michael. Today is Your Day to Win. New York: Michael Brescia
2000

Chiles, James R. Inviting Disaster: Tales from the Edge of Technology. New
York: HarperCollins Publishers, Inc., 2001, 2002
The Power of Positive Investment in Yourself

Hansard, Christopher. The Tibetan Art of Positive Thinking: Skillful

Thoughts for Successful Living. New York: Atria, August 2005

Peale, Norman Vincent. The Power of Positive Thinking. New York:

Random House, Inc., 1952

"Power of a super attitude: Reeve's life bolsters theories on mind-body

health link." USA Today: Sharon Jayson, October 13, 2004, p.

The Power of Positive Investment in Yourself